Carving
Faces
WORKBOOK

Learn to Carve Facial Expressions
with the Legendary Harold Enlow

HAROLD ENLOW

Introduction by Harley Refsal and Roger Schroeder,
former editor of *Woodcarving Illustrated*

FOX CHAPEL
PUBLISHING

© 2011 by Harold Enlow and Fox Chapel Publishing Company, Inc., East Petersburg, PA.

Caving Faces Workbook is an original work, first published in 2011 by Fox Chapel Publishing Company, Inc. The patterns contained herein are copyrighted by the author. Readers may make copies of these patterns for personal use. The patterns themselves, however, are not to be duplicated for resale or distribution under any circumstances. Any such copying is a violation of copyright law.

Pattern drawings by John Allard.

Photo on page 10: Andy Anderson, 1953, Shotgun Wedding, 21.6.11, Stark Museum of Art, Orange, Texas.

ISBN 978-1-56523-585-4

Library of Congress Cataloging-in-Publication Data

Enlow, Harold L.
 Carving faces workbook / Harold L Enlow.
    p. cm.
 Includes index.
 Summary: "Learn to carve faces with Harold Enlow!   Harold Enlow, one of America's foremost caricature carvers shares the woodcarving tips and techniques that make his carvings stand-out in this information packed book. Inside, you'll follow-along as Harold teaches you how to carve faces with life and expression"-- Provided by publisher.
 ISBN 978-1-56523-585-4 (pbk.)
 1. Wood-carving. I. Title.
 TT199.7.E525 2011
 736'.4--dc22
                                    2011000930

To learn more about the other great books from Fox Chapel Publishing, or to find a retailer near you, call toll-free 800-457-9112 or visit us at *www.FoxChapelPublishing.com*.

Note to Authors: We are always looking for talented authors to write new books in our area of woodworking, design, and related crafts. Please send a brief letter describing your idea to Acquisition Editor, 1970 Broad Street, East Petersburg, PA 17520.

Printed in China
First printing: August 2011

About the Author

Harold L. Enlow was born in Missouri, the oldest of nine children in a family that moved frequently, occasionally serving as migrant workers. Harold admired the way his grandfather made things out of wood and says his most memorable childhood gift was a pocketknife from his mother, which he used to carve all the bark off a boxelder tree in the front yard.

"I enlisted in the U.S. Army when I was 17 and spent time in Maryland, New Mexico, and Okinawa, Japan," says Harold. "While in Okinawa, I found a book in the base library by H. S. 'Andy' Anderson and was immediately hooked on caricature carving.

"After being released from the army, I married Elaine. A year later, I was called to serve during the Berlin crisis. While I was serving at Fort Lewis Army Base in Washington, I began to carve seriously. When that tour ended, I returned to Springfield, Missouri, where I met Peter Engler, who owned a shop in Silver Dollar City near Branson, Missouri. I carved for Peter and sold carvings through his shop for a few years before opening my own shop in 1968 in Dogpatch, Arkansas."

The town was named for Dogpatch, U.S.A., an amusement park based on the fictional hillbilly town made famous by Al Capp's comic strip "Li'l Abner." It opened the same year Harold moved there and closed in the mid 1990s.

In 1975 Harold began the second phase of his carving career, teaching his first carving class and seeing his first carving book published. He continued to write and teach up to 40 classes a year for the next three decades, reaching thousands across the United States and Canada. He now has a dozen books and many study sticks to his credit, with subjects ranging from cigar store Indians and Western figures to hillbillies and hoboes.

In 1990 Harold and a number of other prominent carvers met to discuss forming a national organization to promote the art of caricature carving. The result was the Caricature Carvers of America (CCA), which is active in exhibitions, seminars, and compilation books featuring members' work. Harold is currently an emeritus member of CCA.

"Few carvers have received the praise that Harold Enlow has gotten. And fewer still have had their names become household words to those who carve," is how *Woodcarving Illustrated* announced his selection as its inaugural Woodcarver of the Year in 2001. The honor was in recognition of "the respect he has earned from students and fellow carvers alike, the quality of his publications, and the impact his work has had on caricature carving."

Except for 4 or 5 local seminars each year, Harold has now retired from active teaching. He and Elaine still live in Dogpatch, now know as Marble Falls.

Contents

Carving Out a Legacy

I was more than a little nervous before meeting Harold Enlow. Friends and acquaintances had been telling me that he is somewhat of a living legend, a prime mover in getting caricature carvings recognized and accepted as a form of art in the United States. In fact, most anyone doing caricatures today has been influenced through his efforts as an instructor of instructors and students alike.

The day came when I finally met Harold. It was prior to his receiving *Woodcarving Illustrated's* Woodcarver of the Year award at the fourth Open House in March 2001, and I was the presenter. When we got through the obligatory introductions and handshakes, I found a man so self-effacing and downright humble that my fears of inadequacy quickly dispersed. The presentation went well, and he gladly received the plaque as well as a framed citation from the office of Arkansas' governor. He went about his duties as a lecturer and manned his booth with a total absence of fanfare. Weeks afterward, I could still imagine his saying, "Gosh, I don't know what all the fuss is about. I'm just a carver." My response to that is, "Hardly."

This early carving, which Harold created in 1962 from a scrap 2 x 4, is titled *Corporal Niels* and shows signs of his later style.

While his biography includes a stint in the Armed Services, running a shop in Dogpatch, doing commission work, writing ten books on a variety of themes from cigar store Indians and Western figures to hillbillies and hoboes, his greatest contribution may well be his teaching career. Spanning nearly four decades with thousands of students "graduated," that relationship with other carvers has had a profound impact. People come away from the classes with an understanding of how a few simple tools can work magic on a piece of wood. And many of those carvers pass that knowledge on to others. The carving world has been a much better place thanks to Harold's efforts.

Sneakin' Past the Sheriff,
Harold's contribution to the 2007
CCA book *Caricature Carvers Showcase.*

Owing to the amount of influence that Harold has had, rumors have circulated that he was around when the Titanic sank and even when Teddy Roosevelt charged a hill in Cuba. Again, I respond with, "Hardly." A robust man with a sprightly step, Harold is as youthful in spirit as any carver I know, and he's not a day over 62.

Putting that humor aside, I learned that while Harold loves to tell a joke, tease his friends, and carve a humorous caricature, he is serious about and dedicated to his carving. I watched him work, observed how effortlessly he removes wood, listened to him explain what he has learned about anatomy over the years, the improvements he has made in his carvings, and how he looks at people. I was in a good position to see exactly why Harold has been so successful as a teacher.

While hillbillies are favorite subjects—he endows them with misshapen hats, beards, long hair and funny faces—Harold doesn't limit himself to these figures. He is just as comfortable carving a leprechaun, a troll, a cowboy, or even a hunter who shot a cow by mistake. A story is projected through an attitude, a gesture, a pose, or an expression that can be wistful, gleeful, sexy, or downright ugly. He consistently captures the flavor of exaggeration and humor in his carvings. When you look at one of Harold's carvings or compositions, your mind may well start writing a script with these carvings as main characters. The people and animals Harold carves are to be treasured just as much as he is.

~Roger Schroeder, managing editor of
Woodcarving Illustrated, 1991

The Swedish Roots of American Caricature

Some people see more than humor in Harold's carvings. Harley Refsal, for instance, sees shades of Scandinavian-style flat-plane carving.

Refsal is emeritus professor of Scandinavian Folk Art at Luther College in Decorah, Iowa, and, like Harold, a founding member of Caricature Carvers of America.

In a 1999 article for *Woodcarving Illustrated,* Refsal drew a line from Swedish carver Axel Peterson Doderhultarn to Enlow.

Doderhultarn's work was widely circulated in Europe and the United States early in the twentieth century. It seems clear that Doderhultarn's knife-marks-exposed, features-exaggerated work influenced American carver Andy Anderson, Refsal wrote, and Anderson in turn wrote the book that turned young Harold Enlow into a caricaturist.

"He was drawn to, and inspired by, Andy's rough-hewn, minimalist, flat plane style. Sometimes he utilized Andy's themes, sometimes he combined Andy's minimalist style with his own themes," Refsal wrote. He quoted Enlow as saying Anderson's book changed his life: "Clearly, I'm standing on the shoulders of Andy Anderson."

And, Refsal wrote, the trail doesn't end there.

"Virtually all of the CCA members, along with numerous other caricature carvers, who in turn teach seminars and classes themselves, have drawn on Harold Enlow—and indirectly on Andy Anderson—for inspiration."

This Andy Anderson piece shows the distinctive caricature style that initially caught Harold's eye. Andy Anderson, 1953, *Shotgun Wedding*, 21.6.11, Stark Museum of Art, Orange, Texas.

Harold's Hints

■ [On selling your work] Happy people sell ten-to-one over grumpy people. Keep smiling.

■ To carve well you have to carve a lot. You can't expect to carve once a year and accomplish anything. Pick up a piece of wood and a knife every day or two and keep after it.

■ When you make a caricature carving, make it look like someone you'd never pick up hitchhiking.

■ Keep your tools sharp. Too many good carvers give up saying they can't carve, not realizing they can't carve because their tools are dull.

■ Sharp tools are for sissies—push harder (a joke)! I learned this from my friend Roy Kinnaird. If you insist on sharpening, remember there are two main steps. Sharpen until a burr forms on the edge. Then strop or buff the burr off. There are some intricacies, but those are the main steps. A little honing compound on your strop or buffer is always good.

■ If you look at a carving from the profile view, you can see a lot of what you may miss if you look at it straight on.

■ If you see the whole eye when looking at the profile of the carving, you have carved the eye too flat. Since the eyeball should be rounded, you should only see half of the eye from the profile view.

■ There is usually one eye length between your eyebrows as well as your eyes, unless you are a werewolf, which has just one eyebrow that runs all the way across.

■ The mouth, more than any part of the face, enhances the look of a figure.

■ If you hold your hands so that the fingers touch at the end of your nose with palms touching the cheeks, the angle between the hands is about 90 degrees.

Paw's New Hare Piece,
a Harold creation from 1999.

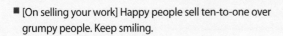

Introduction

You have in your hands a definitive volume that will teach you how to carve realistic and fantastic faces. The projects in this book are available in the form of study stick kits (see page 144 for purchasing information)—however, you don't need to buy a study stick to carve these faces. Just make your own! Go get a stick of basswood, about 1½" x 2" x 16", and embark on creating the faces in this book. At first, you might not get it quite right, but it's easy to turn or flip the stick and try again.

My instructions list the tools I use, but you do not need to use the exact ones I mention; feel free to use whatever you have on hand. What matters is ending up with faces that please you.

Start with the basic building blocks of any face—eyes, lips, nose, hair, and ears. "Carving Facial Features" will show you how to create these essentials, and how to craft variations such as curly hair, bulbous noses, sleepy eyes, and more.

After you've mastered those vital projects, move on to "Carving Complete Faces." You have seven faces to choose from. If you're in a whimsical mood, the wood spirit on page 131 is a fitting and forgiving choice—carve the flowing hair however you'd like. Those of you feeling Christmas-y can try carving your own version of Santa, on page 96. When you've followed along with Harold through all the faces, don't be afraid to put the pieces together and carve your own unique faces. The possibilities are endless!

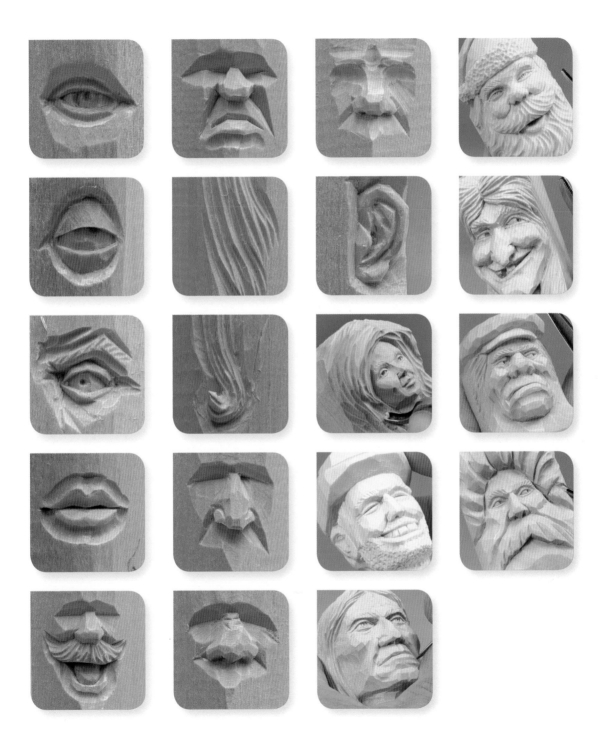

Carving Facial Features

Before you can successfully carve a face, either realistic or caricature, you must learn to create the elements of that face. In this section I will walk you through my tested steps to creating and customizing basic facial features. When we finish, you will be well on your way to transforming plain sticks of wood into engaging characters.

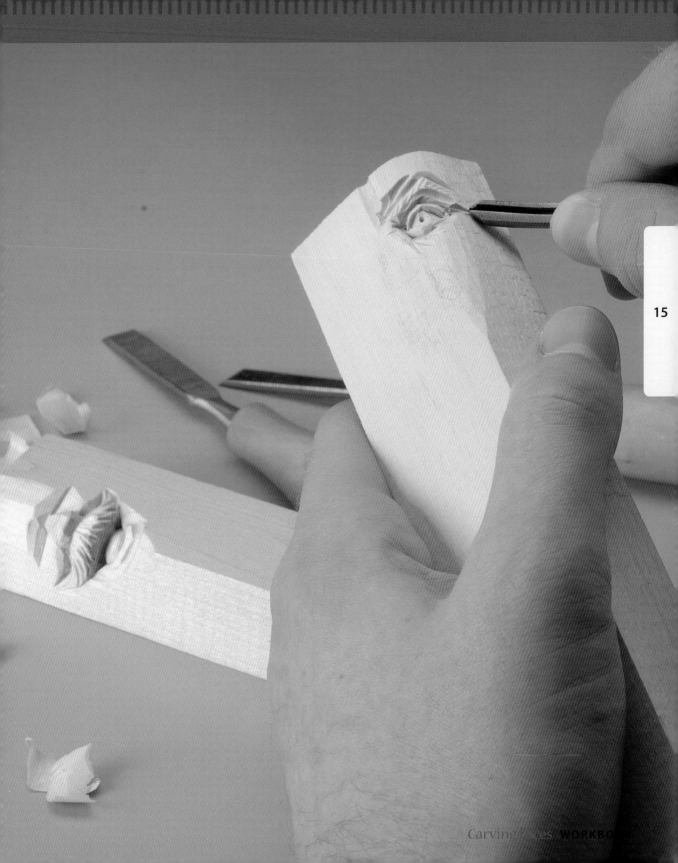

Eyes

They say the eyes are the windows of the soul, and instead of taking the risk and carving an eye, many carvers paint in eyes. But this usually requires a carver to paint his entire carving.

The basic technique to carve an eye is the same for every eye; four V-tool cuts give the basic shape to the eye. You can tailor the shape to the carving based on how deep you make these cuts and how far apart the cuts are. The shape of the iris and pupil affect the mood of the carving.

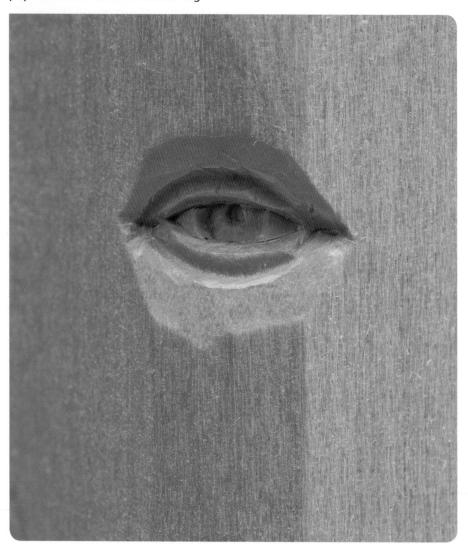

Basic Open Eye

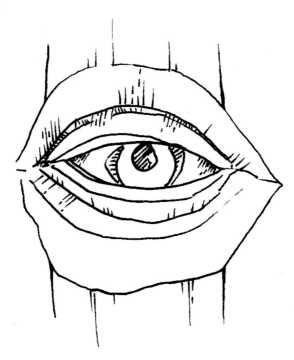

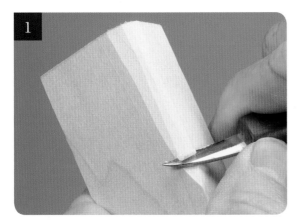

Prepare the blank. Round the corner because eyes are rounded, not flat. Use a carving knife.

Create the brow line. Make a rounded stop cut, cutting deeper at the rounded corner and shallower as you approach the sides with a carving knife. Carve up to the stop cut to create the brow line and eye socket. Repeat the process until you have a fairly deep eye socket.

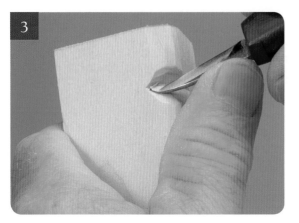

Rough in the eyeball. Remove a triangular chip of wood from the inside and outside corners of the eye with a carving knife. This helps you begin to round the eyeball.

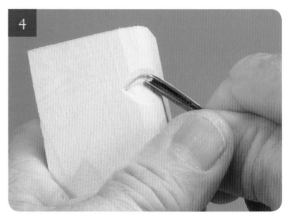

Make the first V-tool cut. Carve the upper eyelid. Carve along the inside crease of the top eyelid with a sharp ⅛" V-tool. This separates the upper eyelid from the eye socket.

Tip: Eyebrows decide the mood.

When carving the eye, you often rough in the shape of the eyebrow. The shape of the face can change based on the eyebrows.

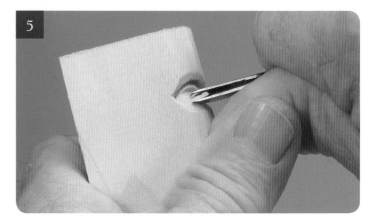

Make the second V-tool cut. Carve the lower eyelid. Carve along the inside crease of the bottom eyelid with a sharp ⅛" V-tool. This separates the lower eyelid from the eyeball.

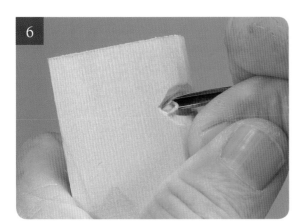

Make the third V-tool cut. Refine the upper eyelid. Carve along the bottom edge of the top eyelid with the wing of the V-tool perpendicular to the eyeball. This separates the upper eyelid from the eyeball.

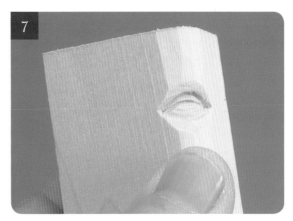

Make the fourth V-tool cut. Refine the lower eyelid. Carve along the top edge of the lower eyelid with the wing of the V-tool perpendicular to the eyeball. This separates the lower eyelid from the eyeball.

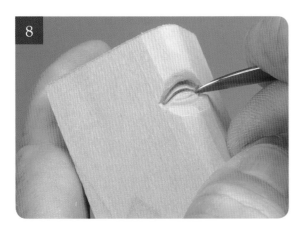

Finish the eyelids. Use a carving knife to thin the lower eyelid slightly so the upper eyelid overlaps the lower lid at the outside corner.

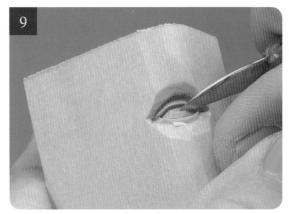

Begin rounding the eyeball. Stop-cut along the edge of the upper eyelid where it meets the eyeball with a detail knife. Cut up to the stop cut and round the eyeball up to the upper eyelid.

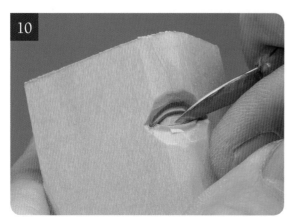

Finish rounding the eyeball. Stop-cut along the edge of the lower eyelid, where it meets the eyeball, with a detail knife. Cut up to the stop cut and round the eyeball down to the lower eyelid. Make sure the upper eyelid sticks out more than the lower eyelid.

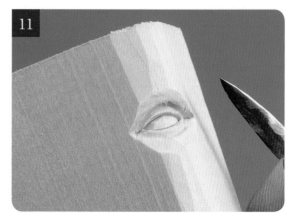

Decide how to finish the eye. If you plan to paint the eye, you are done. If you plan to apply a natural finish, carve the iris and pupil.

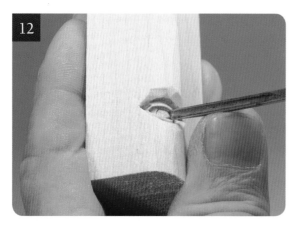

Draw in the iris. Use a small gouge (which fits the curve you've drawn on the eyeball) to outline the iris. This cut will create a shadow, making the iris more distinct.

Carve the pupil. Stab in the pupil with a micro veiner. The whole pupil shows under the upper eyelid. Carve out the pupil using a micro veiner and clean up the pupil with a detail knife. The goal is to create a deep shadow.

Sleepy or Drunk Eye

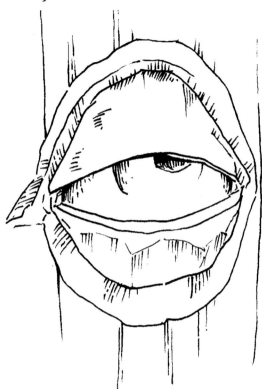

Prepare the blank. Round the corner of the blank because the eyeball is round. Use a carving knife. Carve the outline of the eye with a ¼" veiner.

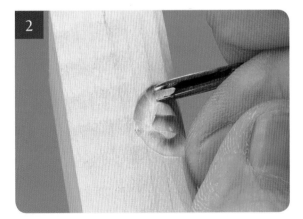

Add the shadows above the upper eyelid. Deepen the groove above the top eyelid with a ⅛" V-tool to create a slight shadow.

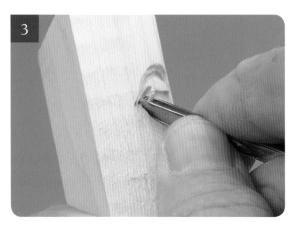

Add the shadows under the lower eyelid. Deepen the groove below the bottom eyelid with a ⅛" V-tool to create a slight shadow.

Carve the upper eyelid. Use a ⅛" V-tool to carve along the bottom edge of the upper eyelid. This separates the upper eyelid from the eyeball.

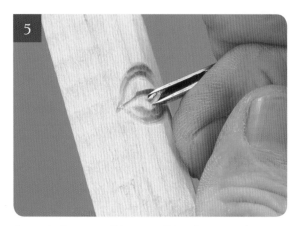

Carve the lower eyelid. Use a ⅛" V-tool to carve along the top edge of the lower eyelid. This separates the lower eyelid from the eyeball.

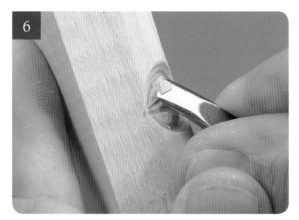

Round the eyelids. Use a ⅜" #3 gouge upside down to round the drooping upper eyelid and the lower eyelid.

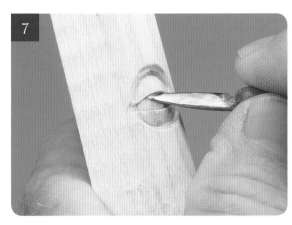

Round the eyeball. Stop-cut along the inside edges of the top and bottom eyelids with a detail knife. Round the eyeball to these stop cuts. Deepen the corners of the eyeball.

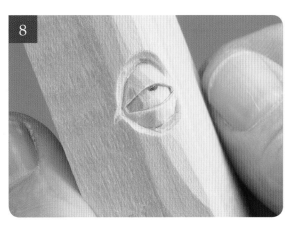

Draw in the pupil. A little less than half of the round pupil is visible below the droopy top eyelid. To make a drunk eye, make the pupil small.

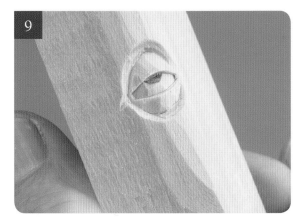

To make a sleepy eye, make a larger pupil.

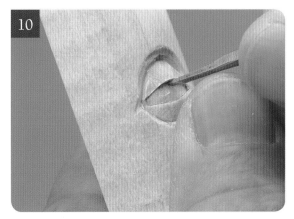

Carve the pupil. Stop-cut in along the pupil line with a micro gouge and free the chip with a detail knife.

Angry Eye

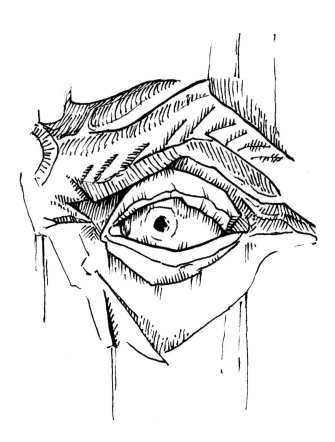

Prepare the blank. Round the corner of the blank with a carving knife. Make a curved stop cut with a carving knife, deeper on the corner and more shallow as it approaches the edges. Carve up to the stop cut to shape the eye socket.

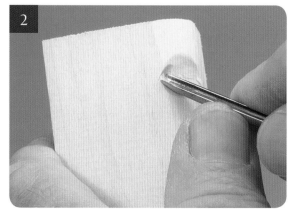

Carve the corners of the eye socket. Carve from the top down and from the bottom up to the inner and outer corners of the eye socket, deepening them with a small gouge. This sets the stage for a round eye.

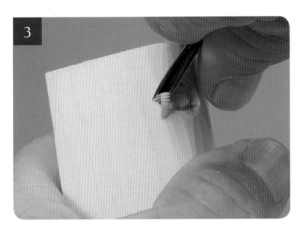

Separate the eyelids from the eye socket. Carve along the deep crease at the top and bottom of the eyelids with a ⅛" V-tool to separate the upper and lower eyelids from the eye socket.

Separate the eyelids from the eyeball. Carve along the bottom of the upper eyelid and the top of the lower eyelid with a ⅛" V-tool. This separates the eyelids from the eyeball.

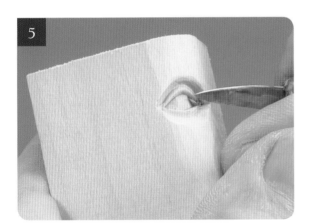

Round the eyeball. Stop-cut along the upper and lower eyelids with a carving knife. Carve up to the stop cuts to separate the eyeball from the eyelids and round the eyeball up to the stop cuts with a detail knife.

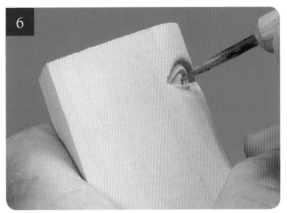

Carve the pupil. Use a micro gouge to carve the pupil. Make the shadow for the pupil even deeper by poking the pupil with an awl.

26

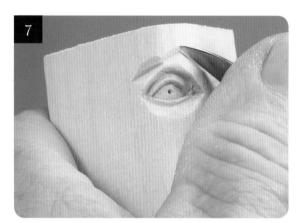

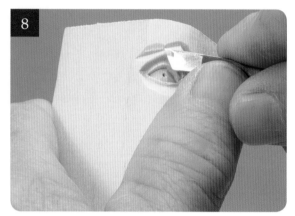

Rough in the angry eyebrow. The eyebrow enhances the angry look of the eye. Stop-cut along the brow line with a carving knife. The brow is furrowed on the inside and arched over the eyeball. Cut up to the stop cut so the brow sticks out a little bit.

Refine the brow. Smooth and refine the brow with a skew chisel.

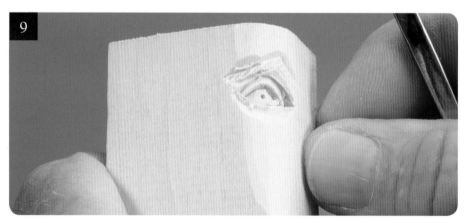

Finish carving the eyebrow. Deepen the brow lines with a ⅛" V-tool. Use the same tool to carve in the eyebrow hair. Refine the edges of the eye with the same tool.

Lips

Lips can say a lot about a person and a person's mood. Smiling lips suggest happiness; thin lips suggest anger or fear. The opening between the lips can also affect the look of the carving.

Most of the time, a woman's lips will be fuller and smoother than a man's lips. The exception is for an older woman, where the lips will end up thin. Men have all sorts of shapes of lips. Regardless of how much space there is between the lips, or if you carve a few visible teeth between the lips, the lips are carved using the same techniques.

Woman's Lips

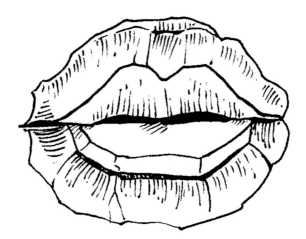

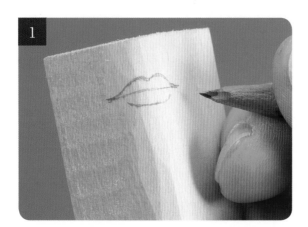

Prepare the blank. Round the corner of the blank and smooth the area for the lips with a carving knife. Because women have smoother skin, the area must be smooth. Draw in the lips. The top lip is usually wider than the bottom lip.

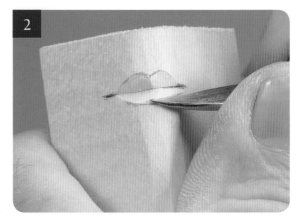

Carve the area between the lips. Make an angled stop cut along the area between the lips with a carving knife. The curve of the blade makes this cut curve on both sides as you press it into the rounded wood. Taper the upper lip from the top of the lip down to the center cut. Use the same technique to shape the bottom lip, tapering up to the center cut.

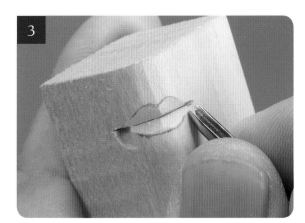

Shape the corners of the lips. Carve up alongside the bottom lip to the top lip with a 3mm veiner. Cut the chip free with the veiner or a detail knife.

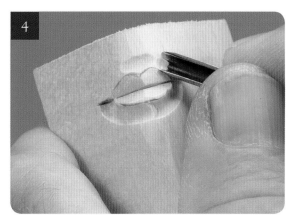

Outline the upper and lower lips. Carve above the upper lip and under the lower lip with a 3mm veiner. The upper lip is slightly pointed and the lower lip is more rounded.

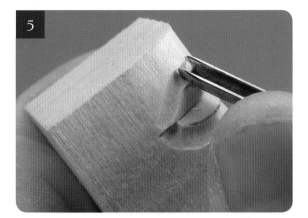

Carve the angel's kiss. Use a 3mm veiner to carve the slight groove between the top lip and the bottom of the nose.

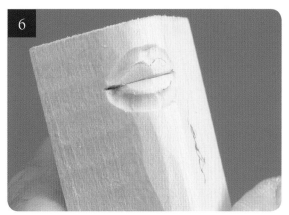

Continue rounding the lower lip. Use a ³⁄₁₆" skew chisel.

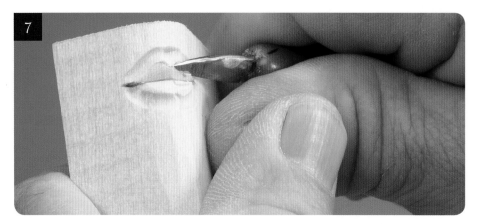

Shape the center of the top lip. Create the rounded pouty top lip using a carving knife.

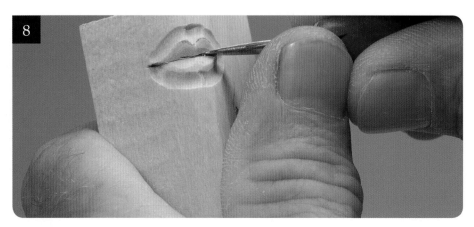

Deepen the area where the lips meet. This area is the deepest part of the carving. Make a deep cut at a slight angle from the top with a carving knife. Then cut up to the stop cut from the bottom to create a thin deep groove.

Lips with Mustache

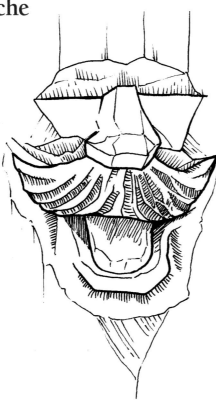

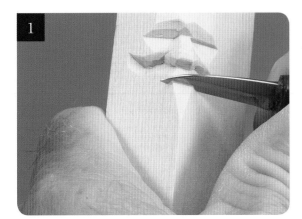

Prepare the blank. Round the corners of the blank and draw in the mustache and bottom lip. I carve in a few rough facial features to give the mustache context. Make a stop cut in the bottom center of the mustache with a carving knife.

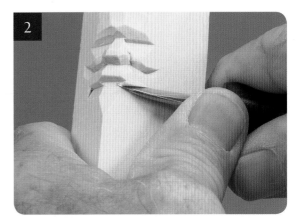

Carve the bottom of the mustache. Cut up to the stop cut. Then make a stop cut along the entire bottom edge of the mustache and cut up to the stop cut to shape the bottom of the mustache.

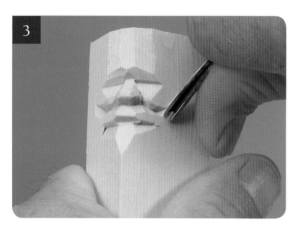

Outline the edges of the mustache. Carve along the edges of the mustache with a ⅛" V-tool.

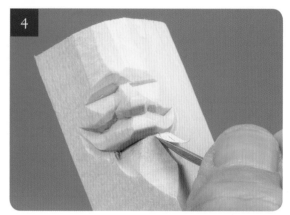

Rough in the corners of the mouth. Make a deep stop cut into the corner of the mouth with a small veiner. Cut the chip free with a carving knife. Round the mouth area with a ⅜" #3 gouge.

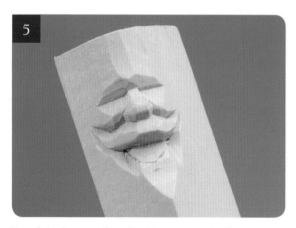

Rough in the mouth cavity. Use a carving knife to deepen the mouth cavity area. Then draw in the corners of the mouth and sketch in the bottom lip.

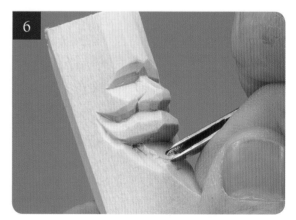

Separate the lip from the mouth. Carve along the pencil lines with a ⅛" V-tool to separate the lip from the mouth. Shape the outside of the lip with a 3mm #5 gouge. The lip thins as you approach the outside corner of the mouth.

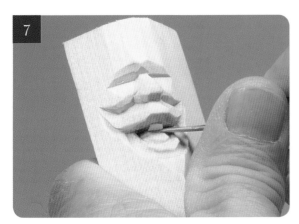

Separate the tongue from the roof of the mouth. Carve a deep groove at the top of the tongue so it looks as if the tongue extends down the throat. Use a detail knife.

Separate the tongue from the lower lip. Make a stop cut between the tongue and the lower lip. Cut up to the stop cut to separate the tongue from the lip.

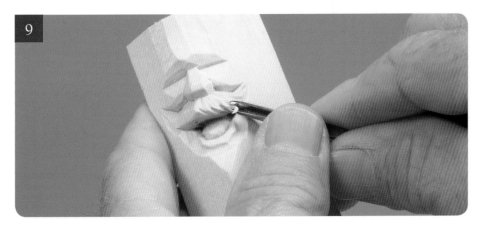

Texture the mustache. Carve a series of grooves with a ⅛" V-tool. Rotate your wrist as you carve the grooves to make curved cuts. Carve a few grooves into the bottom of the mustache with the same tool to break up the flat surfaces. Clean out any fuzzies with a denture brush.

Frowning Lips

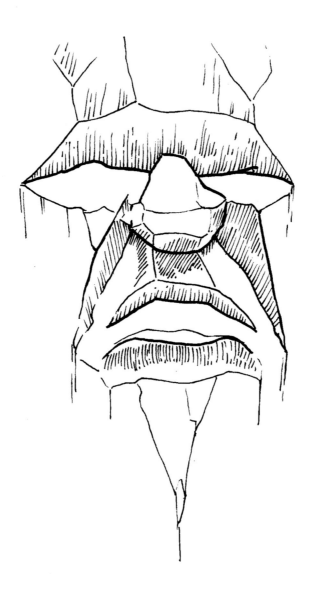

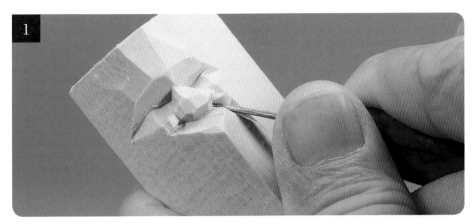

Carve the frown lines. Rough in the nose to give the mouth context. A pouty mouth needs deep frown lines to convey the emotions. Carve deep frown lines from the corner of the nose downward. Round over the sharp corners with a ⅜" #3 gouge.

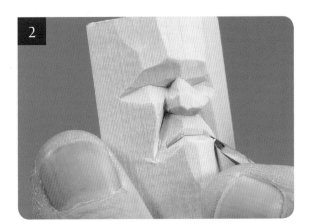

Shape the lips. Make a stop cut between the lips and taper the upper lip down to the stop cut. Then taper the lower lip up to the stop cut. Make sure the lower lip sticks out. Round the upper lip with a ⅜" #3 gouge.

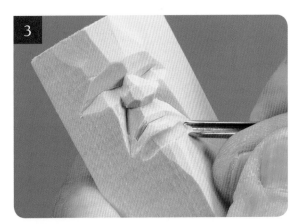

Shape the lower lip. Carve under the lower lip with a 3mm #5 gouge to separate the lip from the area under the lip. Use the same tool to refine the shape of the lower lip. Round the lips with a skew chisel or detail knife.

Hair

Most carvings will include some sort of hair, whether it is hair on the head, a mustache, or a beard. Hair is one place where you can introduce a bit of realism to make the caricatured parts stand out.

Basic hair is really only a series of carved grooves. There are a few more steps to carving a curled lock, or curlicue, of hair. I use a V-tool for men's hair because it looks more rugged. It can also look stringier. For women's hair, I use a small #11 gouge. This gouge, also called a veiner or U-gouge, allows you to carve more flowing locks of hair.

Basic Hair

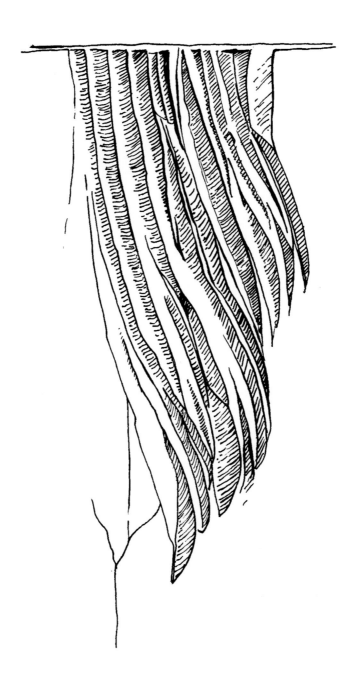

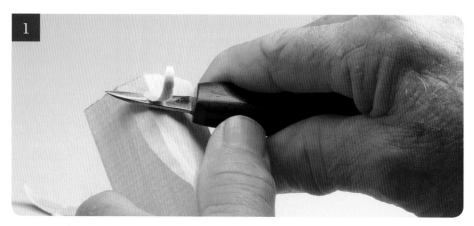

Round the corner of the blank. Hair wraps around the head, so the base under the hair should be round. Use a carving knife.

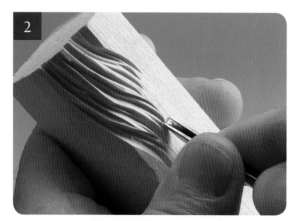

Carve the hair. For a man's hair, carve a series of curved lines with a ⅛" V-tool. Use a small veiner to carve a woman's hair. Make sure there are no straight lines. Straight lines look too static. Eliminate flat spots by carving between two nearby hairs wherever there is a flat spot. Deepen some cuts to create more shadow.

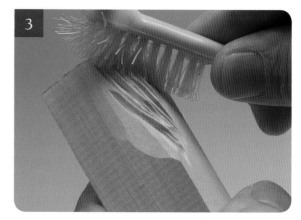

Clean out the fuzzies. Use a denture brush to scrub out any small fuzzies. Make light cuts with the V-tool to clean up any rough cuts.

Curly Hair

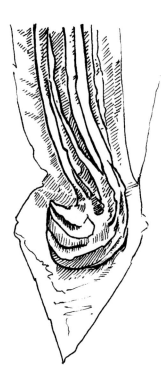

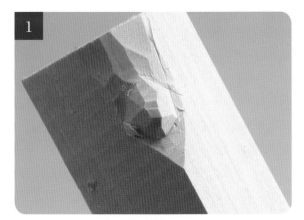

1

Carve an oblong lump. I call this carving a grape. Round the corner of the block. Make a stop cut above and below the curl and cut up to the stop cut to separate the curl from the background hair. Round the edges of the curl to make the oblong lump.

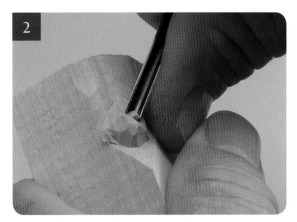

2

Carve the center of the curl. I call this "making a doughnut." Use a small veiner to carve a groove in the top left quadrant of the lump.

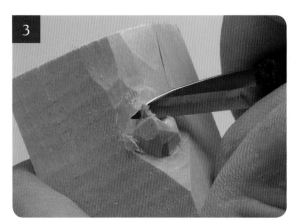

Carve the area where the curl overlaps. I call this "making a lock (split) washer." Make a stop cut on one side of the doughnut with a carving knife. Carve up to the stop cut to separate the tip of the curl from the rest of the hair. This creates a visible curl on the end of the lock of hair.

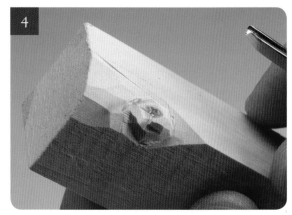

Create the curl. Use a ⅛" V-tool to undercut the edges of the top curl and to rough shape the sides of the curl. Then use the same tool to begin carving some lines representing hair into the curl. Start at the curl and work up toward the top of the blank.

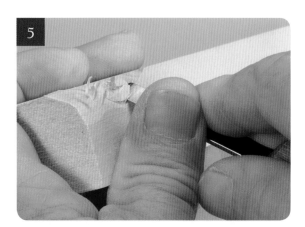

Separate the curl from the background. Make a stop cut around the curl with a ¼" #3 gouge. Cut up to the stop cut with the same tool to isolate the curl from the rest of the hair.

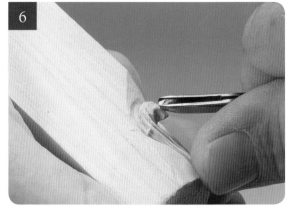

Refine the hair texture. Use a ⅛" V-tool. Carve around to the tip of the curl. Be careful when you are cutting across the grain because the wood will be more fragile and you can break away the hair texture. Use a denture brush to remove any fuzzies.

Noses

Looking at most faces, the most prominent feature is the nose. The shape of a person's nose is usually unique to that person, which makes it difficult to mess up a nose; you can always reshape it a bit to fix a mistake.

One thing to remember about noses is that they stick out from the face more than any other feature. Noses are technically half in the face and half sticking out from the face. If you were to place a 90° square on your face, the nose would touch the angle of the square and the sides of the square would rest on your cheeks.

Pointed Nose

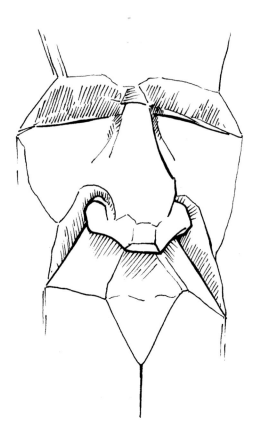

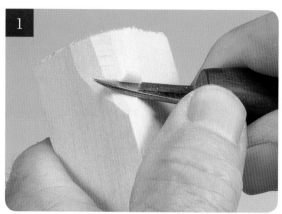

Prepare the blank. Since the nose sticks out the most from the face, use the corner of the blank as the centerline of the nose. Round the forehead above the eye line with a carving knife to give the nose context.

Rough in the eye sockets. Make a stop cut along the eye line and carve up to the stop cut with a carving knife. This determines the position of the eye sockets and the saddle of the nose. The saddle is the thinnest part of the bridge of the nose between the eyes. Use the carving knife to deepen the eye sockets near the nose to separate the eyes from the bridge of the nose.

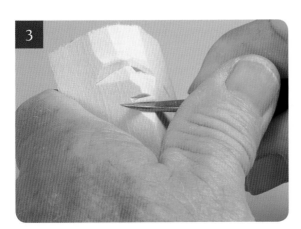

Rough out the bottom of the nose. Stop-cut along the bottom of the nose with a carving knife. Cut up to the stop cut to remove a wedge of wood from under the nose. This separates the tip of the nose from the rest of the face.

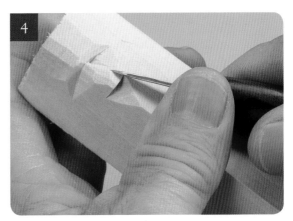

Separate the nose from the cheeks. Stop-cut along the side of the nose and cut up to the stop cut to separate the nose from the cheeks. Half of the nose sticks out from the face and the other half of the nose is in the plane of the face.

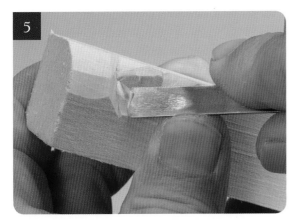

Shape the cheeks. Use a ⅜" #3 gouge to carve away wood from the cheeks up into the eye sockets. Use the same tool to shape the side of the nose as you deepen the eye sockets. Start with the right side of the nose if you are right-handed and the left side of the nose if you are left-handed. That way, you can make the nose symmetrical on both sides.

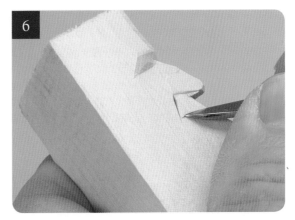

Refine the bottom of the nose. Make a stop cut at the bottom corner of the nose and cut up to the stop cut to rough-shape the bottom of the wings of the nose. This also roughs out the smile lines.

Carving Faces **WORKBOOK**

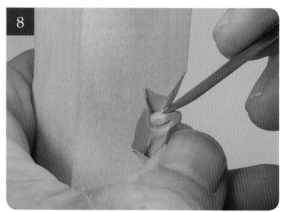

Shape the top of the nose wings. Carve in the groove that separates the wings of the nose from the main part of the nose. Use a ⅛" V-tool.

Carve the nostrils. Turn the carving upside down to carve the nostrils. Stab in with a ⅛" #5 gouge for both nostrils. Cut up to the stab cut with a detail knife to free the chip.

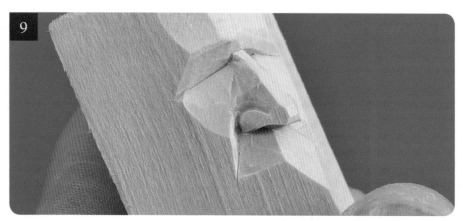

Refine the shape of the nose. Round over any sharp corners with a carving knife. Refine any rough areas using the same tool.

Wide Nose

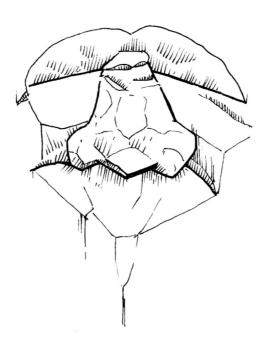

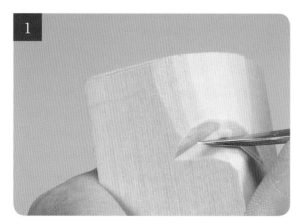

Prepare the blank. Round the forehead area and make a stop cut along the eye line with a carving knife. Cut up to the stop cut to rough in the eye sockets.

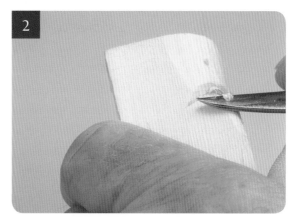

Widen the saddle of the nose. Since this will be a wide nose, you need to increase the overall thickness of the nose. Otherwise, the eyes will look like they are too close together compared to the bulbous nose.

Rough out the bottom of the nose. Make a stop cut along the bottom of the nose with a carving knife. Cut up to the stop cut to separate the nose from the mouth.

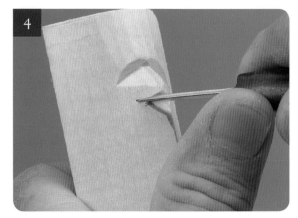

Outline the edges of the nose. Stop-cut along the side of the nose and cut up to the stop cut with a carving knife. This roughs in the wide squished nose.

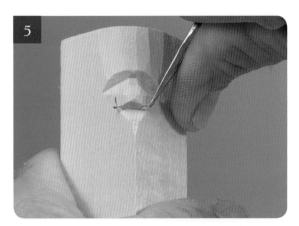

Define the outer corners of the nose. Use a ³⁄₁₆" skew chisel and a carving knife. Stop-cut along the outer corners of the nose. Then cut up to the stop cuts to set the nose back into the plane of the face.

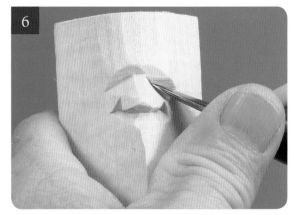

Refine the cheeks and side of the nose. Carve alongside the nose up into the eye sockets. Because I am right-handed, I use a knife on the right side of the face and a ³⁄₈" #3 gouge on the left side of the face. Deepen the eye sockets with a skew chisel.

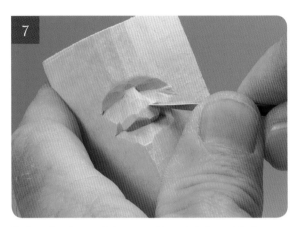

Refine the shape of the nose. Use a ³⁄₁₆" skew chisel to round and shape the sides of the nose.

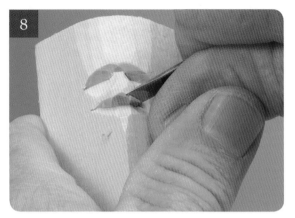

Refine the sides of the bottom of the nose. Use a ³⁄₁₆" skew chisel to round and shape the bottom of the nose.

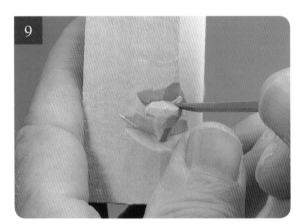

Carve the nostrils. Stab in with a ⅛" #5 gouge on both sides of the septum, or flap of skin between the nostrils. Cut up to the stab cut with a detail knife to free the chip.

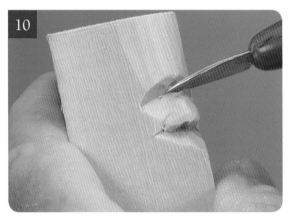

Finish the nose. Remove any fuzzies with a denture brush. Carve a few wrinkles onto the top of the nose with a detail knife.

Bulbous Nose

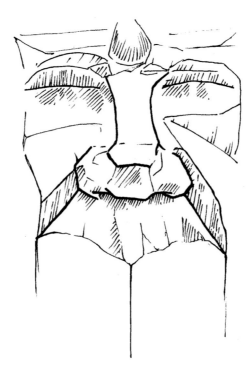

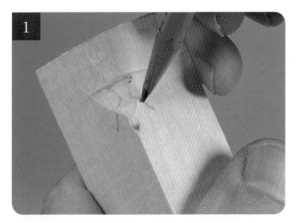

Prepare the blank. Round the forehead and make a stop cut straight across the blank at the eye line. Carve up to the stop cut to rough shape the eye sockets. Draw in an hourglass shape to represent the outside shape of the nose.

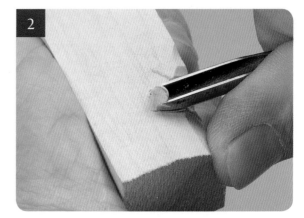

Deepen the eye sockets. Use a ¼" #11 gouge, or veiner, to carve deep eye sockets. Use the same tool to reduce the thickness of the bridge of the nose.

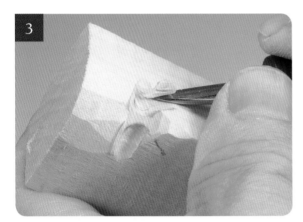

Shape the cheeks. Stop-cut along the lines. Use a carving knife on the right side and a skew chisel on the left side. Cut up to the lines to separate the cheeks from the nose. Deepen the eye sockets even more with a ¼" veiner.

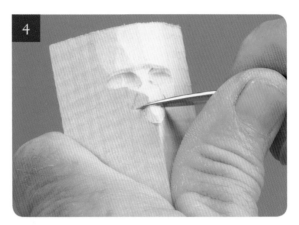

Shape the bottom of the nose. Stop-cut along the bottom of the nose with a carving knife. Then cut up to the stop cut to separate the nose from the mouth area with a carving knife. Refine the tip of the nose and the cheeks with a carving knife.

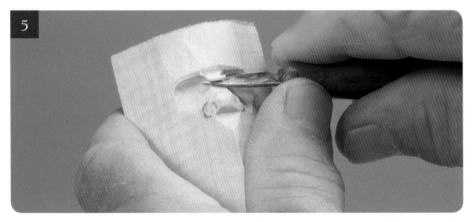

Shape the bridge of the nose. Draw in the wings of the nose. Thin the bridge of the nose with a detail knife and ⅜" #3 gouge. Make the nose look like a ski jump.

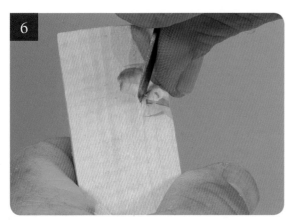

Shape the sides of the nose. Stop-cut along your lines with a ⅜" #3 gouge and cut up to the stop cut to separate the edge of the nose from the face and to set the nose back into the plane of the face.

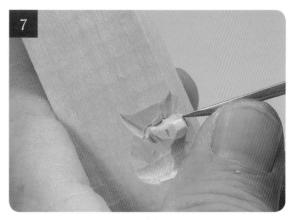

Carve the nostrils. Stab in on both sides of the septum with a ⅛" #5 gouge. Cut up to the stab cuts with a detail knife. Carve the wings of the nose with a V-tool.

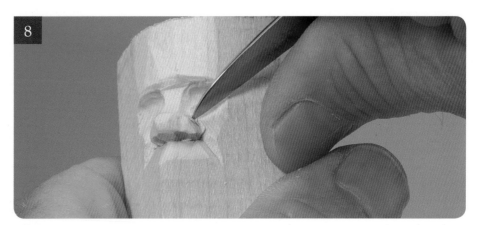

Finish shaping the nose. Deepen the eye sockets and shape the bridge of the nose with a ¼" veiner. Refine the overall shape of the nose and remove the sharp corners with a detail knife.

Ears

While it's easy to hide an ear behind a lock of hair or under a hat, ears allow you to add a great deal of character to a carving. Ears are simple enough to carve, and like most other features, easy to fix if you make a carving misstep.

On a realistic carving, an ear reinforces the carver's ability to create an image in wood. On a caricature carving, the ears are easy to exaggerate and undersized ears or oversized ears add to the joke of the carving. While you can make the ears oversized, the carving will look better if you carve the same basic structure as a realistic ear.

Basic Ear

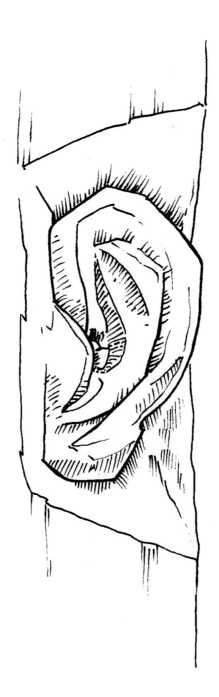

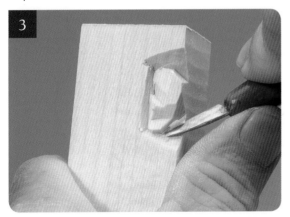

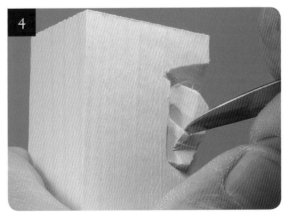

Outline the ear. Draw in a rectangle for the ear. Make a stop cut along the top of the rectangle with a carving knife and cut down to the stop cut. Make a stop cut on the bottom of the rectangle and cut up to the stop cut with a carving knife. Make a stop cut on the outside line of the rectangle with a ⅜" #3 gouge and cut up to the stop cut.

Add the notch to the bottom of the ear. Use a carving knife to taper the top outside edge of the ear. Then carve the notch into the side of the ear with a carving knife.

Shape the outside bottom corner of the ear. Round the outside bottom corner of the ear with a carving knife.

Shape the tragus. The tragus is the little flap of skin sticking out of the ear near the face. Stop-cut around the tragus with a carving knife and cut up to the stop cut so the tragus sticks out.

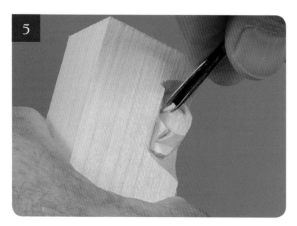

Shape the inside edge of the ear. Carve along the inside edge of the ear with a ⅛" V-tool.

Deepen the area around the tragus. Use a ⅛" V-tool to deepen the area around the tragus. This creates a realistic shadow around the tragus.

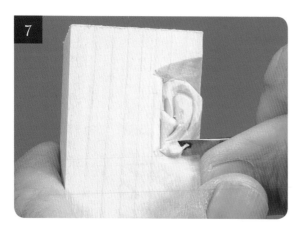

Round the edges of the ear. Use a ³⁄₁₆" skew chisel or a carving knife.

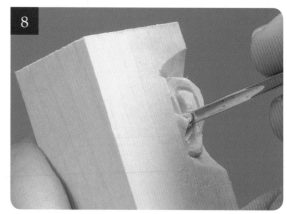

Carve the hole in the ear. Make a deep cut with a ⅛" #5 gouge. The hole is positioned just behind the tragus.

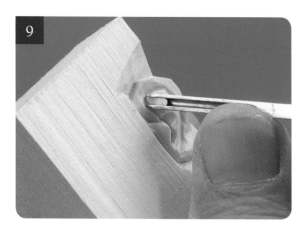

Shape the inside of the upper ear. Use a 2mm veiner to carve the Y at the top of the ear. Refine the area and round over the sharp corners with a micro gouge and a detail knife.

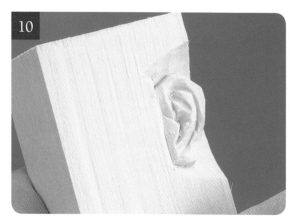

Finish shaping the edges of the ear. Use a ³⁄₁₆″ skew chisel and a carving knife to refine the overall shape of the ear and to round over any sharp edges.

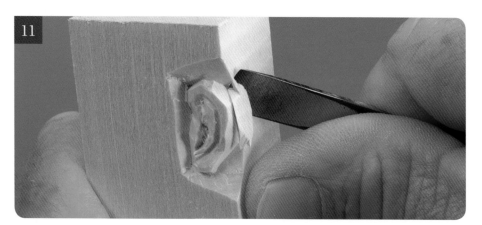

Undercut the back of the ear. Use a ³⁄₈″ #3 gouge to undercut the back of the ear. Refine the back of the ear with a carving knife.

Carving Complete Faces

Now that you have some practice carving facial features, it's time to move on to a new challenge—entire faces. What you learned on the individual elements will help, but your education doesn't end there. Each face you complete will teach you more about how to effectively make your wooden creations look the way you want them to.

Female Face

A beautiful woman's face intimidates many carvers. The perception is that it's easier to carve a man's face, or an ugly woman's face. But if you take your time, it's just as easy to carve a beautiful woman's face as it is to carve any other face.

Remember that the overall bone and muscle structure is the same for all women. Gravity, age, and a little bit of genetics are all it takes to turn a beautiful woman's face into a less attractive one. If you learn to carve a beautiful woman's face, it's simple to thin the lips, add a few wrinkles, or reduce some of the thickness of the cheeks to age the woman or tone down her beauty.

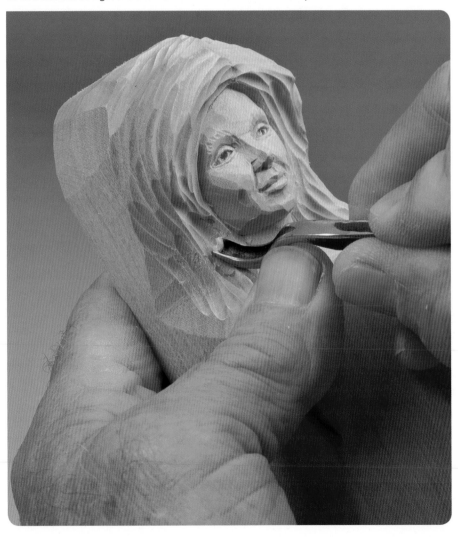

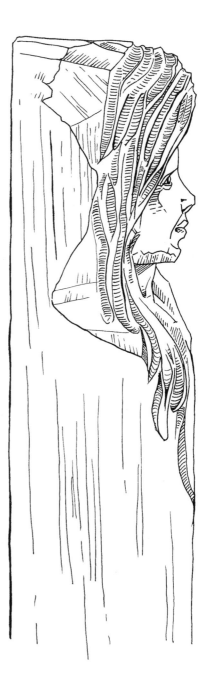

Carving Faces WORKBOOK

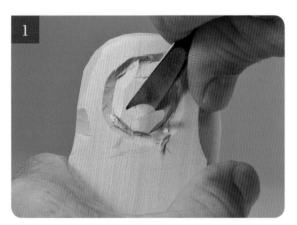

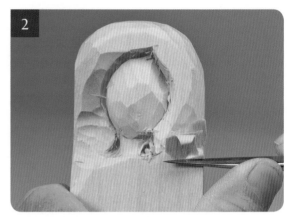

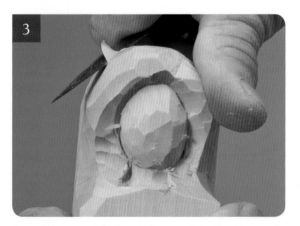

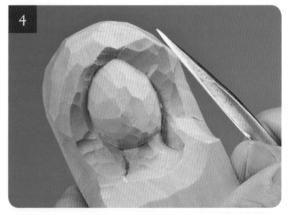

Begin shaping the face. Stop-cut around the hairline with a ⅜" #3 gouge. Taper the forehead up to the hairline with the same tool. Carve from the hairline in toward the sides of the face and under the chin. Flip the same tool upside down to round the face down to the stop cut.

Carve down the hair on the sides of the neck. Use a carving knife and a ¼" veiner. Use the veiner to rough in the neck. Carve a slender neck on women; if you leave a thick neck on a woman, she looks like a football player. Continue to round the face down into the hairline with a ⅜" #3 gouge.

Round the top of the head. The top of the head is round, so the hair over the head should be round. Remove some of the bulk from the top of the hair with a carving knife.

Continue setting in the face. Rough in the face until the face and neck are separated from the hair. Use a carving knife. The hair should flow back from the forehead down to behind the neck.

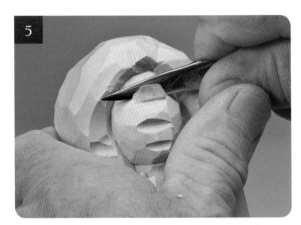

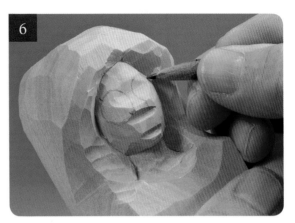

Begin carving the profile. Use a 3mm veiner to carve in the bottom of the nose and the lips. Stop-cut along the brow line with a carving knife and taper the forehead to this stop cut. The base of the nose and top of the nose should make a 90° angle so the nose turns up slightly.

Sketch in the sides of the nose and the eye sockets. I draw two circles to represent the eye sockets and sides of the nose. It gives the nose an hourglass shape that flares up into the brow line.

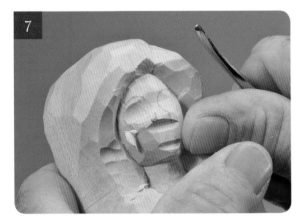

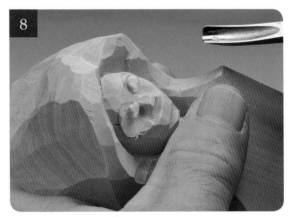

Rough in the eye sockets. Use a ⅜" #9 gouge to carve out the eye sockets and separate the sides of the nose from the eye sockets.

Shape the eye sockets. Round away the sharp corners on the cheeks with a ³⁄₁₆" skew chisel. Carve alongside the nose with the ⅜" #9 gouge to shape the side of the nose.

61

Carving Faces **WORKBOOK**

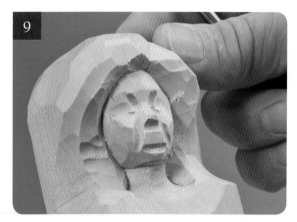

Carve the smile lines. Carve down alongside the nose with a 3mm veiner to begin shaping the cheeks.

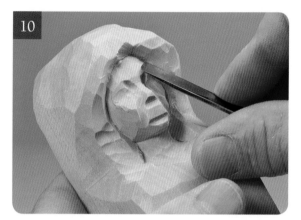

Continue shaping the face. Carefully use a #3 gouge to round the forehead and clean up any areas around the hairline. For a beautiful woman, the forehead and eye sockets/nose must be smooth.

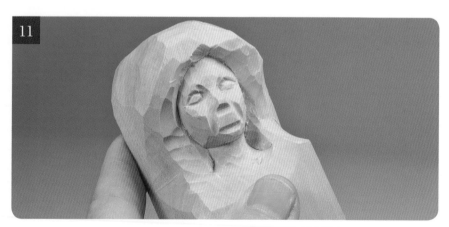

Begin carving the eyes. Use a ⅛" V-tool to separate the top and bottom eyelids from the eye socket. Create a football shape. Match the two eyes up. Deepen the corner of the eye closest to the nose with a 3mm veiner. Use a skew chisel to round the outside brow bone and cheek into the eye socket.

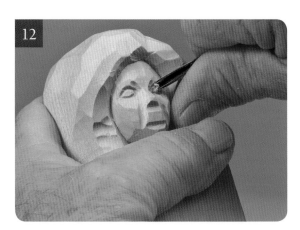

Carve the eyelids. Deepen the corner of the eye closest to the nose with a 3mm veiner. Use a ³⁄₁₆″ skew chisel to round the outside brow bone and cheek into the eye socket. Stop-cut along the eyelids with a detail knife.

Shape the eyeball. Use a skew chisel and a detail knife to carve up to the stop cuts to round the eyeball between the eyelids.

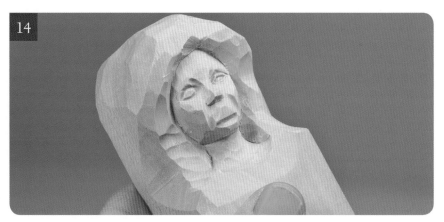

Shape the smile lines. Use a detail knife to round the edges of the smile lines and shape the cheek and chin area alongside the nose and under the mouth.

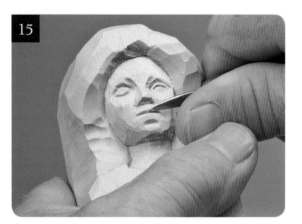

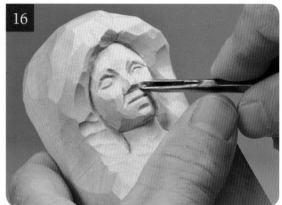

Shape the nose and mouth. Carefully shape the area alongside the nose with a ³/₁₆" skew chisel and a carving knife. Then carefully cut between the lips and round the lips down into the cut between the lips with a carving knife.

Reestablish the smile lines. Use a ⅛" V-tool to deepen the smile line grooves. The smile lines end just above the wings of the nose.

Refine the nose and brow line. Carefully round the nose up to the saddle with a carving knife. Round the brow line using a ⅜" #3 gouge.

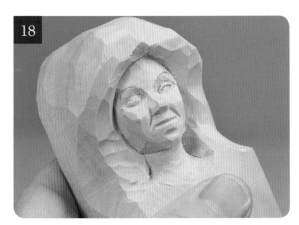

Sketch in the eyebrows. The circles drawn earlier are only the rough shape of the eye sockets. Refine the overall shape of the eyebrows to make bright, large, open eyes.

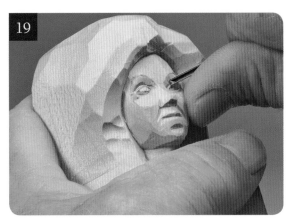

Round the eye sockets. Use a ³⁄₁₆" skew chisel to carve out a little wood between your pencil lines and the eye sockets. This opens the eye up and gives the carving a wide-eyed innocent look. Carve a deep groove to separate the upper eyelid from the eye socket with a small V-tool.

Tip: Delicate Features.

Since women's features tend to be more delicate, it's important to clean up your carving. Nothing spoils the illusion of a beautiful woman's face more than large rough cuts. Make many small cuts rather than a few large cuts.

Deepen the corners of the eyeball. Use a carving knife and a ⅛" V-tool. This helps add shadow and helps make the eyeball appear round under the eyelids. Use a detail knife to carefully smooth and round the eyeball.

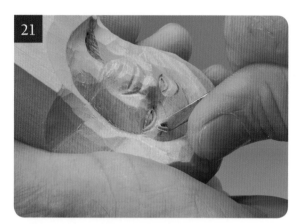

Refine the eye sockets. Use a ³⁄₁₆" skew chisel to round the brow line down into the eye socket. Use a ⅛" V-tool to deepen the corners of the eyes and shape the top of the cheeks.

Refine the lips. Round the lips with a detail knife. Use a micro veiner to carve the corners of the lips and to carve under the bottom lip.

Carve the angel's kiss. Use a micro gouge to carve the groove up the center of the area between the top lip and the nose.

Refine the bottom of the nose. Square off the edges of the bottom of the nose with a detail knife to make the nose stick up a little more.

Begin carving the iris. Use a micro gouge to stop-cut around the outside of the iris.

Finish carving the iris. Recess the wood of the iris slightly lower than the eyeball, using a detail knife.

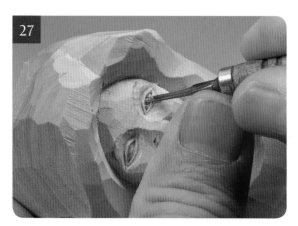

Carve the pupil. Carve up and in to the pupil using a micro gouge. Cut the chip free using a detail knife.

Refine the nose. Use a detail knife to shape the nose. Try to create a slightly pointed tip that sweeps up a bit.

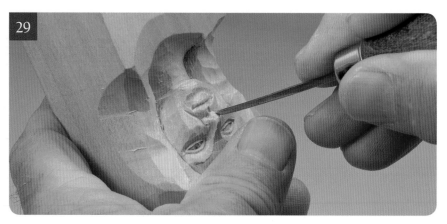

Carve the nostrils. Use a micro gouge to carve straight into the nose. Cut the chip free with a detail knife.

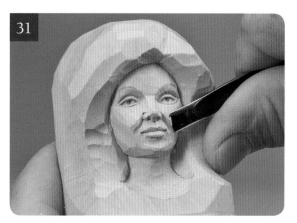

Shape the cheeks. To make the woman look to be in her mid-20s, thin her cheeks slightly using a detail knife and a ⅜" #3 gouge. To make a teenager or younger girl, keep the cheeks round.

Continue rounding the face. Use a ⅜" #3 gouge upside down to smooth and round the face.

Carve the dimples. Use a 3mm veiner to carve in the dimple grooves.

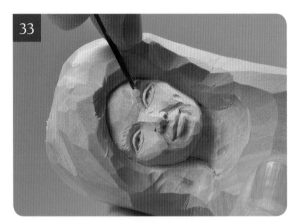

Carve the eyebrows. Use a micro-gouge to carve a series of lines representing the eyebrows.

Carve the hair. Carve a series of grooves with a 3mm veiner. I use a gouge to carve a woman's hair as it creates a softer, more feminine look.

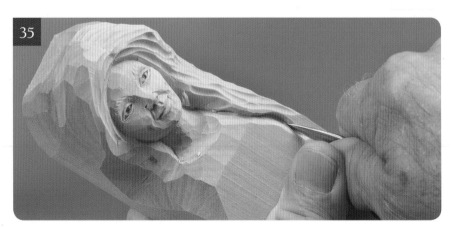

Carve the ends of the hair. Separate the locks of hair from the rest of the block. Make a deep groove with a carving knife.

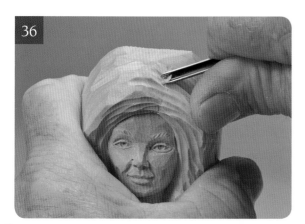

Separate the hair at the part. Carve grooves out from both sides of the part using a 3mm veiner. Carving out from both sides of the part defines the part without creating an unnatural hard line.

Clean up the fuzzies. Scrub the hair with a denture brush to remove any fuzzies.

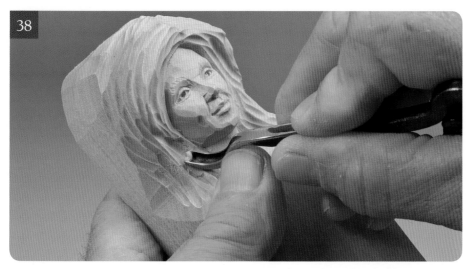

Carve the hair in the deep area next to the neck. I use a shopmade short-bent veiner to rough out the hair in the deep area where the grain changes direction abruptly. Clean up the area with a 3mm veiner.

Cowboy

Cowboy caricatures have a long history in America, dating back to the classic work of Andy Anderson, who is credited as one of the earliest American caricature carvers. Even today, broken-down cowboys find their way into almost every carving competition and most popular instructors offer rough-outs of cowboys.

As with most caricatures, the success of the carving depends on a blend of realistic and exaggerated features. Most good caricature artists realize that you need to know how to create a realistic face in order to do a good caricature. It doesn't take much to turn a realistic carving into a caricature. On this cowboy, the ears are a little oversized and the teeth are slightly larger than normal. Both of these features give the carving a fun and happy look.

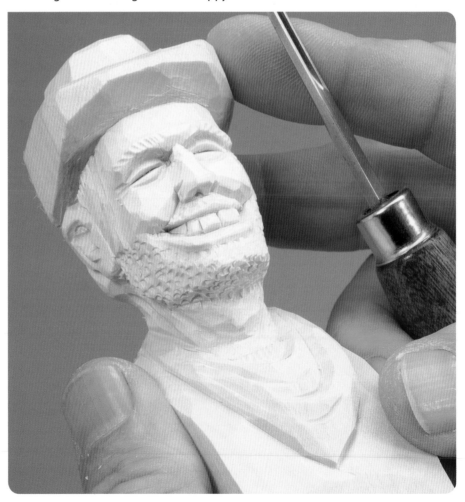

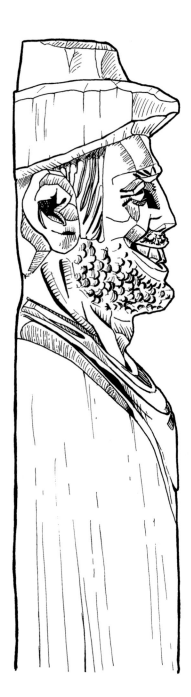

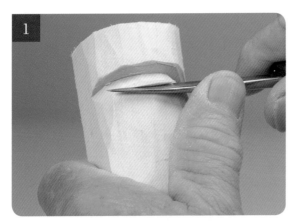

Rough in the hat. Round the top of the blank. Stop-cut along the bottom of the hat line with a carving knife and carve up to the hat line to begin shaping the forehead. If you were carving a cowboy figure, the hat brim would naturally be wider than the one shown on the study stick.

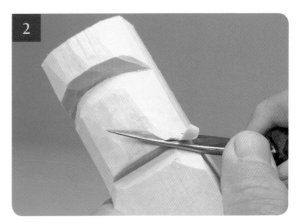

Separate the chin from the neck. Stop-cut along the chin line with a carving knife and carve up to the stop cut to separate the chin from the neck. Begin to round the face. Leave wood in the middle of the face for the nose.

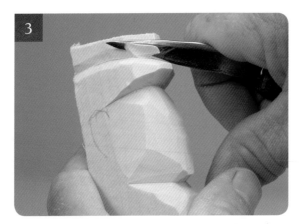

Rough out the top of the hat. Stop-cut along the top of the hat brim with a carving knife and carve up to the stop cut. Continue removing wood until you establish the large brim and small crown of the hat.

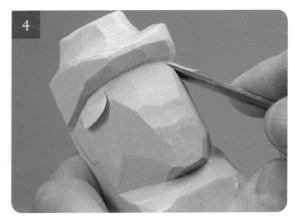

Rough in the sides of the face. Carve a notch around the hat brim on top of the ears. Then carve away the wood in the temples and in front of the ears with a ⅜" #3 gouge.

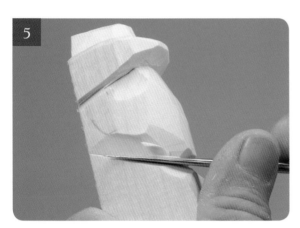

Remove the wood under the ears. Use a carving knife.

Shape the sides of the head. Taper the sides of the face toward the chin using a carving knife. Then thin the temple area to make the nose stick out more.

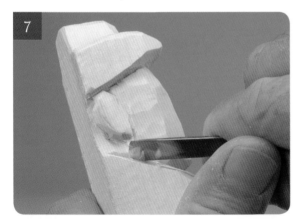

Rough in the ears. Use a #3 gouge to carve up alongside the ears to separate the ears from the face. Carve around the ears to isolate the ears from the rest of the head. The backs of the ears stick out more than the front of the ears, which blend into the sides of the face.

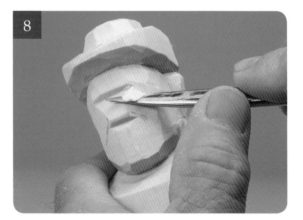

Outline the major facial features. Stop-cut along the brow line and at the bottom of the nose with a carving knife. Carve up to these stop cuts. The cut up to the brow line shapes the top of the nose. The cut up to the bottom of the nose begins to shape the bottom lip. Extend the cut along the brow line and rough in the eye sockets.

Carving Faces **WORKBOOK**

Rough in the nose. Stop-cut alongside the nose with a carving knife and cut up to the stop cut to separate the nose from the cheeks.

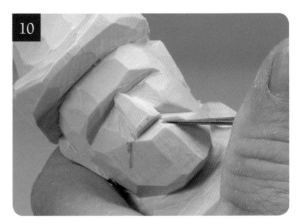

Add the smile lines. Stop-cut along the smile lines with a carving knife. Cut up to the stop cuts to free a wedge of wood to represent the smile lines.

Rough in the mouth and chin. Stop-cut along the cleft of the chin with a carving knife and carve down to the stop cut to create the mouth mound.

Add the sideburns. Sketch in the sideburns. Stop-cut along the sideburn with a ⅜" #3 gouge and then cut up to the stop cut to separate the sideburn from the face.

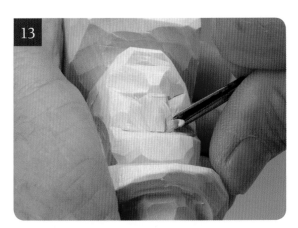

Separate the eyelids from the eye sockets. Carve along the inside corner of the eyelids using a V-tool to separate the eyelids from the eye sockets. Deepen the inside corner of the eye socket near the nose.

Clean up the eyes. Use the tip of a carving knife to clean up the eyelids and eye socket.

Add the wings to the nose. Outline the wings with the tip of a carving knife and carve up to the stop cut to free the chip. This separates the wings of the nose from the cheeks.

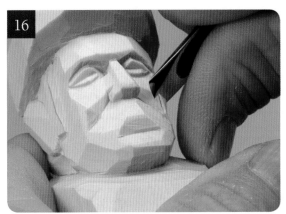

Round over the cheeks. Use a ⅜" #3 gouge upside down or a carving knife to round over the cheeks.

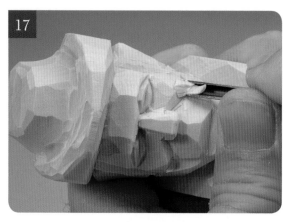

Finish shaping the cheeks. Deepen the smile lines using a 3mm veiner.

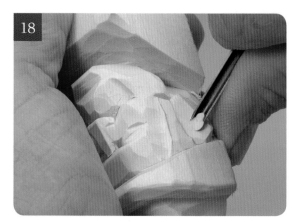

Carve the hole in the ears. Push and rotate a 3mm veiner in a circle to carve a small hole in the ears.

Carve under the ear. Use a knife to remove wood from under the ear to make the lobe of the ear stick out.

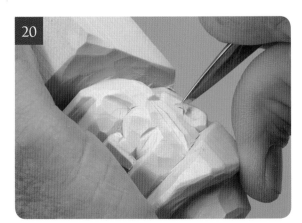

Carve the inside of the ear. Stop-cut along the internal structure of the ear. Taper your cuts inward so the cuts meet in the middle and free the chip.

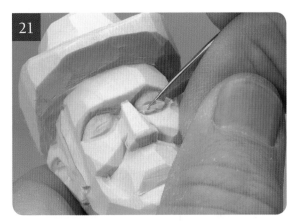

Round the eyelids. Since the cowboy is squinting, and there is very little iris and pupil visible, the eyelids will cover most of the eye. Use a carving knife to round the eye down into the bottom of the V-tool cuts.

Rough in the mouth. Shape the mouth mound under the nose with a ⅜" #3 gouge. Draw in the line between the lips and carve along the line with a ⅛" V-tool.

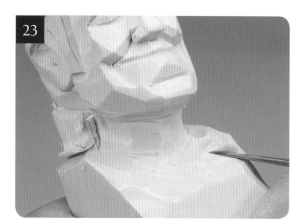

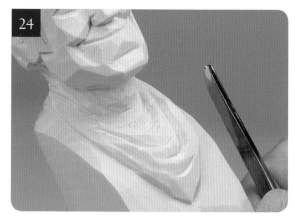

Rough out the neck and chin. Use a carving knife, a veiner, and a ⅜" #9 gouge to remove the excess wood around the bandanna and the neck. Separate the chin from the neck and the neck from the bandanna.

Add the bandanna wrinkles. Draw in a series of J-shaped and reverse J-shaped lines. Carve along the lines with a ⅛" V-tool. Use a carving knife to recess the base of the neck area. Clean up the wrinkles with a ³⁄₁₆" skew chisel. Carve the grooves representing the visible T-shirt collar with a ⅛" V-tool.

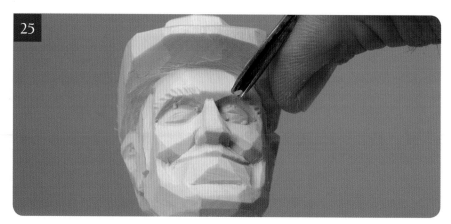

Carve the eyebrows. Carve a series of short lines with a ⅛" V-tool. Use the V-tool to add a few crow's feet.

Carve the squinting eyes. Carve between the eyelids with a small V-tool to create the squinting eyes. Deepen the cuts with a carving knife.

Carve the mouth. Stop-cut along the top lip and the bottom lip with a carving knife. Carve up to the stop cuts to separate the teeth from the lips. The deepest part is the corners of the mouth. Carve under the lower lip with a 3mm veiner to shape the lower lip.

Carve the teeth. Use the tip of a carving knife to carve small grooves to represent the teeth and the gaps between the teeth.

Finish carving the ear. Use a V-tool to carve the remaining grooves inside the ear.

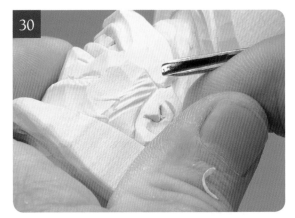

Carve the sideburns. Use a V-tool to carve hair texture into the sideburns. Make sure the lines are curved.

Carve the whiskers. Carve across the grain with a micro gouge. Make short strokes. Push the gouge in and pop out the wood. Make sure you do not carve them into regular rows. Carve the tiny grooves randomly. Carve all over and under the chin. Then carve whiskers over the upper lip.

Native American Chief

Native American faces have long been popular carving subjects. Native American facial features are distinct enough that it's worth learning to carve one.

One thing I like about Native American faces is that you don't need to worry too much about refining the features. The rougher and craggier the features, the more grizzled and world-weary the carving looks. If you refine the features, the carving turns into a young brave warrior. The intent of this project is to demonstrate how to carve realistic features, but after you understand what the features should look like, it's easy to exaggerate some features to transform it into a caricature.

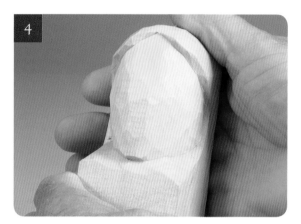

Rough in the face. Round the face up to the nose and down to the hairline. Use a carving knife. Round the face down from the nose to the forehead and the chin using a carving knife.

Carve the eye line. Mark the eye line and stop cut along the saddle of the nose, which is the top of the bridge of the nose, with a carving knife. Cut up to the stop cut with a carving knife. Notice the sloped forehead.

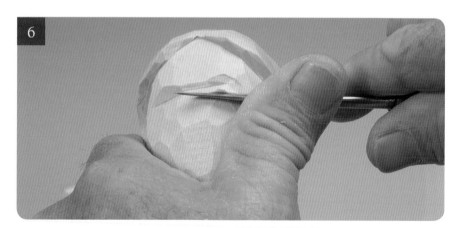

Add the brow lines. Extend the stop cut for the eye line out on both sides of the nose with a carving knife. Carve up to the stop cut with a carving knife to create the brow line and eye sockets.

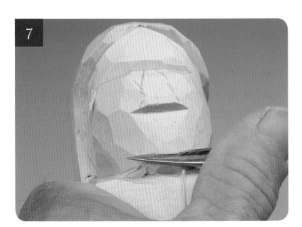

Rough in the nose. Draw in the nose. Stop-cut along the bottom of the nose with a carving knife and cut up to the stop cut to separate the nose from the lips.

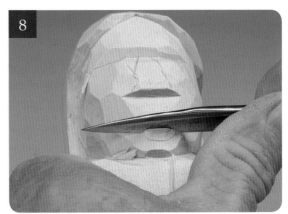

Define the edges of the face. Make a stop cut under the chin and cut up to the stop cut with a carving knife. Round the edges of the face. Carve a shallow landmark groove to establish the position of the brow line.

Tip: Distinctive Facial Features.

The slope of the forehead should match the slope of the nose. When you draw a line from the chin to the nose, both lips should touch that line.

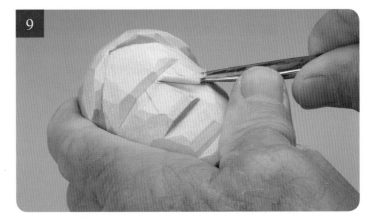

Refine the nose. Stop-cut alongside the nose with a carving knife to separate the nose from the cheeks. Then, position your knife on the cheekbone with the blade facing toward the eye. Push the tip up to the inside corner of the eye while slicing out toward the side of the face to free the chip.

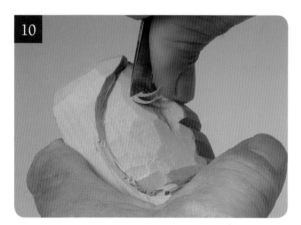

Deepen the eye sockets. Use a ⅜" #3 gouge. This separates the bridge of the nose from the eye sockets. Carve from the cheek up toward the brow. Use the same gouge to carve in along the brow line and remove the chips.

Deepen the corners of the eye sockets. Carve from the center to the inside corner of the eye socket on the top and bottom with a ⅛" V-tool to deepen the inside corner of the eye. Then carve from the center out on the top and bottom to deepen the outside corner of the eye.

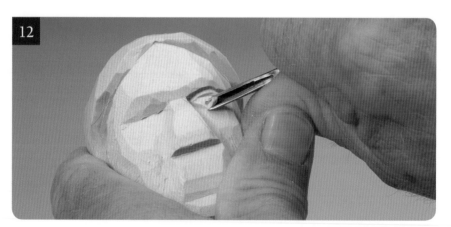

Separate the eyelids from the eye sockets. Carve along the inside corner of the top and bottom eyelids with a ⅛" V-tool. This groove separates the eyelids and eyeball from the eye sockets.

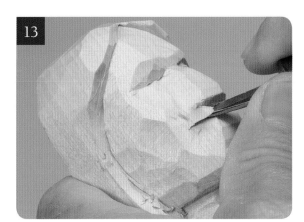

Carve the mouth mound. Use a carving knife to carve up to the nose from below to shape the mouth mound.

Outline the corners of the nose. Mark the corners of the nose and make a stop cut straight in with a carving knife. Cut up to the stop cut to free the chips.

Separate the eyeball from the eyelids. Carve along the eyelids with a ⅛" V-tool. Make sure the eyes match. You may need to remove a little wood from the top or bottom of one eye to make it match the other eye. Use the tip of a carving knife or a V-tool.

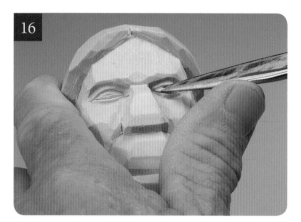

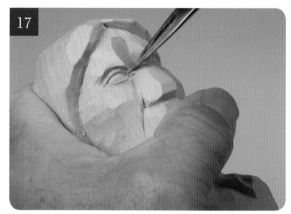

Round the eyeball. Use the tip of the knife to round the eyeball up to the eyelids. From the side you should only see to the center of the eye. If you see the inside corner of the eye, use the tip of the knife to carve the corner deeper.

Refine the nose. Use a carving knife to round and shape the sides of the nose. Carve up alongside the nose with a ⅛" veiner to shape the saddle of the nose and the bridge of the nose.

Refine the tip of the nose. Round the tip of the nose with a ⅜" #3 gouge. Use the same gouge to round the mouth mound up to the nose.

Shape the chin. Use a 3mm #6 gouge to smooth and shape the chin structure.

Rough in the mouth. Carve along the line between the two lips with a ⅛" V-tool. Carve from the center outward on both sides.

Carve the wings of the nose. Use a ⅛" V-tool to carve the shallow groove representing the wings of the nose on both sides of the nose.

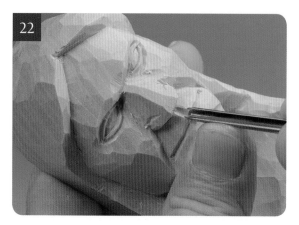

Carve the angel's kiss. Cut from the top of the upper lip to the center of the bottom of the nose with a ⅛" #5 gouge. Cut the chip free with a detail knife.

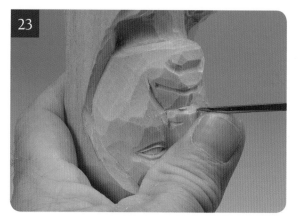

Carve the nostrils. Turn the carving upside down. Stab in with a ⅛" #5 gouge on both sides of the septum (the flap of skin between the nostrils). Cut the chips free with a carving knife.

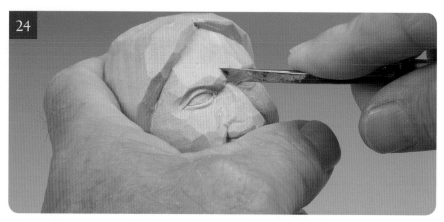

Add wrinkles to the face. Carve the separation between the eyebrows with a ³⁄₁₆" skew chisel. Carve some wrinkles between the brows with the same tool, then add a few wrinkles to the nose.

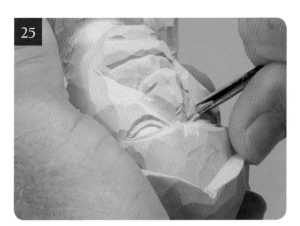

Carve the bag under the eye. Carve a groove under each eye with a ⅛" V-tool. Carve up to the V-tool groove with a ⅜" #3 gouge. Use the ⅛" V-tool to add crow's feet to the corners of the eye.

Add the brow ridges. Use a carving knife to carve the top of the brow ridges. This separates the brow from the forehead. Carve the eyebrow hair with a ⅛" V-tool.

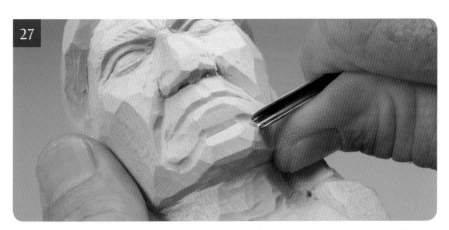

Finish shaping the lip. Carve under the lower lip with a ⅛" veiner. Use the same tool to refine the shape of the lower lip.

Shape the cheekbones. The cheekbones run upward at a slight angle. Use a ⅜" #3 gouge and a carving knife to separate the cheekbones from the rest of the face.

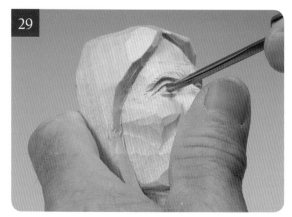

Carve the irises. Stab in the outline of the iris with a ⅛" #5 gouge. Use the tip of the carving knife to recess the iris slightly.

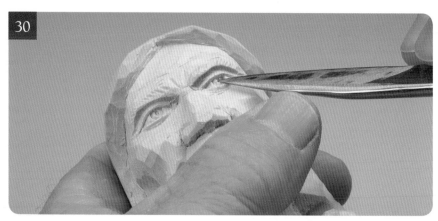

Carve the pupils. Stab up and in with a micro veiner. Cut the chip free with a carving knife.

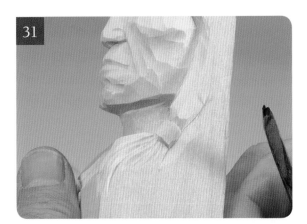

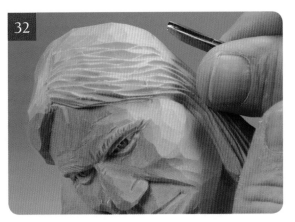

Rough in the hair. Make a stop cut on either side of the hair band and carve up to the stop cuts to separate the hair bands from the hair using a ³⁄₁₆" skew chisel. Carve the two parts of the hair. Undercut the hair and hair band using a ³⁄₈" #3 gouge. Round the hair band with a ³⁄₁₆" skew chisel.

Carve the hair texture. Use a ⅛" V-tool to carve the grooves representing the hair. Then use a carving knife to shape the neck framed by hair.

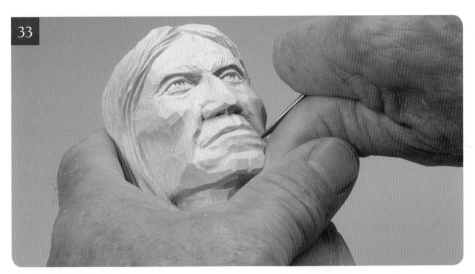

Deepen the line between the lips. Cut down at a slight angle into the opening between the lips with a carving knife. Cut up to the stop cut from below to deepen the opening between the lips.

Santa

Santa is one of the best-loved and most popular carving subjects. The classic Coca Cola Santa, based loosely on cartoonist Thomas Nash's drawings, has inspired generations of carvers. This Santa is a mixture of realistic features with a few exaggerated features that pay homage to the classic poem, "A Visit from St. Nicholas."

After you master the basic techniques of carving this Santa, you can adapt the features and elements to create your own unique St. Nick. Most of the facial features that make this Santa look kind and jolly can also be adapted to other carvings where you want to illustrate those feelings.

Rough in the top. Sketch in the major landmarks, such as the nose, fur trim of the hat, and hat pom-pom. Carve the rough shape of the top and remove a few chips from alongside the face to rough in the hat with a carving knife.

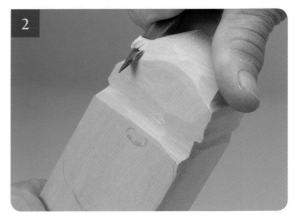

Taper the top. The nose is the highest point of the carving, so taper the top of the face and head down a bit to make the nose stick out. Use a carving knife.

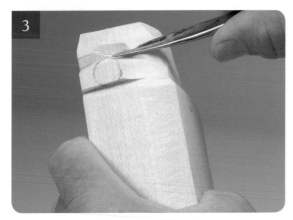

Isolate the hat pom-pom. Sketch in the hat pom-pom and carve above and below the ball with a carving knife.

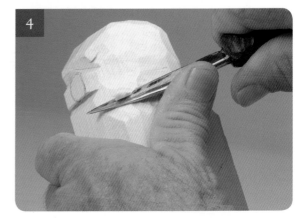

Rough in the overall shape of the face. Use a ⅜" #9 gouge to remove the excess wood around the facial features. Remove the deep gouge marks with a carving knife.

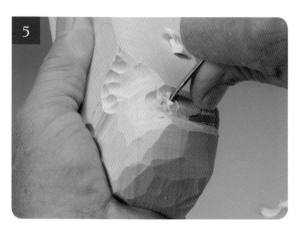

Stop-cut around the hat pom-pom. Stab in with a ⅜" #3 gouge and cut up to the stop cuts to further isolate the hat pom-pom.

Separate the top of the hat from the tail of the hat. Use a ⅜" #3 gouge to carve the top of the hat.

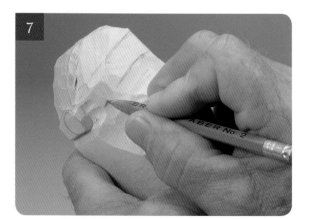

Sketch in the fur trim. Draw the top and bottom of the fur trim.

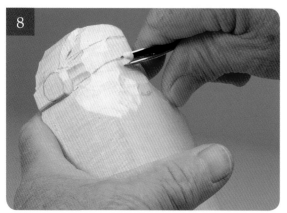

Separate the fur trim from the face. Carve just under the bottom of the fur trim line with a ¼" veiner. Then carve above the top trim line using the same tool.

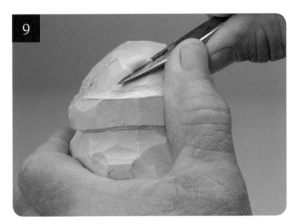

Round the top of the hat. Use a carving knife to round the top of the hat above the line carved in Step 8.

Taper the forehead. Carefully taper the forehead up to the gouge line cut in Step 8. You may need to deepen the cut with a carving knife to free the chips.

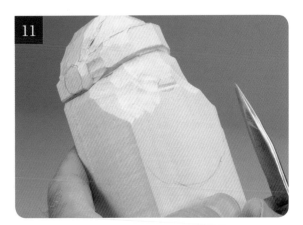

Outline the bottom of the nose. Make an angled cut under the nose using a carving knife. This defines the bottom of the nose.

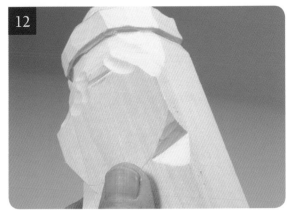

Rough in the bottom of the beard. Carve deep wedges of wood out from both sides under the beard. This Santa has a round bushy beard and these cuts establish the bottom of the beard.

Round the hat pom-pom. Use a ⅜" #3 gouge upside down to round the hat pom-pom.

Further isolate the nose. Use a ¼" veiner to remove wood from under and around the nose so the nose sticks up even more.

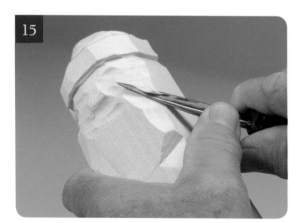

Round the face. Use a small veiner, a ⅜" #3 gouge, and a carving knife to outline the bottom of the beard.

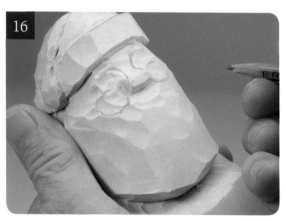

Sketch in the nose and eye sockets. The nose is hourglass-shaped. Then draw in the puffy round cheeks.

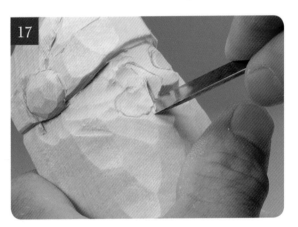

Separate the nose from the cheeks. Use a ⅜" #3 gouge. Stop-cut along the cheek line and carve from the nose up to the stop cut.

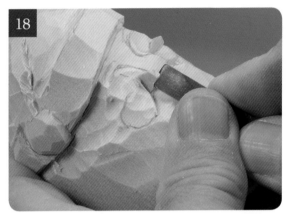

Shape the nose. Smooth off the bottom of the nose and use the #3 gouge upside down to round over the edges of the nose. Use a skew chisel to rough in the wings of the nose.

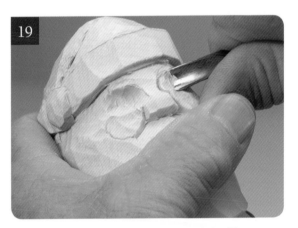

Rough in the eye sockets. Use a ⅜" #9 gouge. The eye sockets run from the bridge of the nose to the outside of the face.

Carve the temples. Use a ⅜" #3 gouge to stop-cut along the temple area. Then carve up to the stop cut to free the chip. Deepen the eye sockets with the ⅜" #9 gouge.

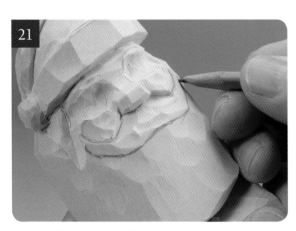

Draw in the mustache. The mustache covers the top lip and runs from the cheeks to the beard and lower lip area.

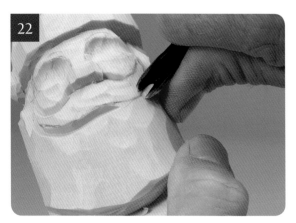

Rough in the mustache. Carve along the mustache lines with a V-tool to separate the mustache from the beard. Use a gouge to lower the area under the mustache where the lower lip will be located.

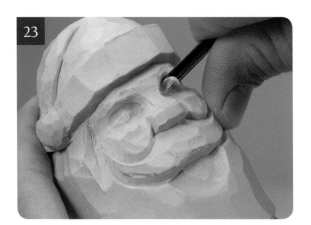

Rough in the eyes. Use a 3mm veiner to deepen the eye sockets. The deepest part of the eye is the inside corner near the nose.

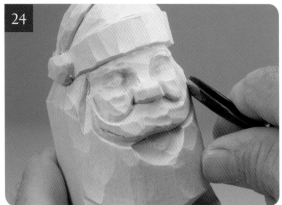

Round the edges of the mustache. Use the side of a V-tool to round the edges of the mustache and the cheeks.

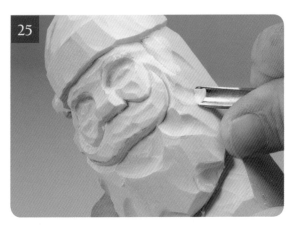

Rough in the beard. Use a ⅜" #9 gouge to break the beard up into large locks of hair. Do not carve any straight lines.

Rough in the lower lip. Rough out the outside corners of the lower lip. Use a 3mm veiner. Then draw the inside of the mouth.

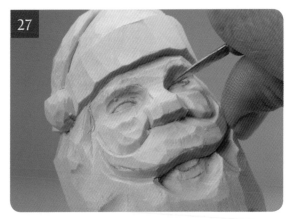

Separate the eyelids from the eyeball. Draw in the football-shaped eyes. Stop-cut along the eyelids with a detail knife. Then carve up to the stop cuts to separate the eyelids from the eyeball. Begin to round the eyeball.

Shape the nose. Use a ⅜" #9 gouge to thin the sides of the nose.

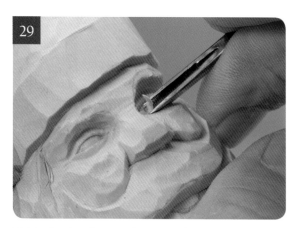

Finish shaping the eyes. Use a V-tool to carve around the upper and lower part of the eyelids to separate the eyelids from the eye sockets.

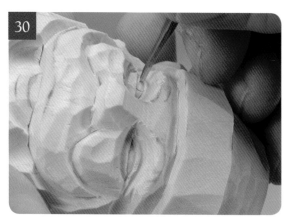

Carve the irises. Stab in with a micro gouge to shape the outside of the iris. Carefully cut up to this stop cut from the inside to create a thin groove around the outside of the iris.

Tip: Carving Eyes.

Carve the Santa's right eye—the left eye as you look at it—first. That way you can see the eye to match it as you carve the Santa's left eye.

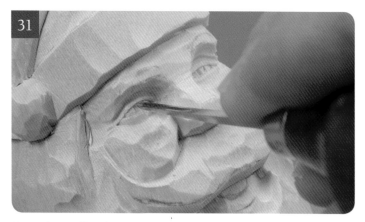

Carve the pupil. Stab up and in with an even smaller gouge. Free the chip with a detail knife.

Carve the ermine fur. Carve a series of short grooves using a 3mm veiner. I use a short push, twist, and popping motion. Make sure the grooves are random; do not make them in regular rows.

Carve the mustache hair. Start on the outside and rotate your hand around like a clock as you carve grooves representing whiskers. Work toward the center where you should have rotated your wrist 180°. This gives the mustache a flowing and realistic texture. Continue the grooves down over the edge of the mustache to the mouth.

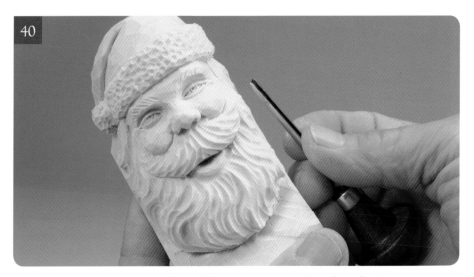

Carve the beard. Carve a series of curved lines using a 3mm veiner. Carve flowing texture between the locks of hair created earlier. Use the same process to carve the sideburns and visible hair.

Witch

While I call this a witch, it could easily be any sort of old ugly woman. You can give her a few more teeth and turn her into an old pioneer woman. Or add a beard or mustache and transform her into a circus performer.

Most of this carving depends on understanding how gravity and age affect the face. The hooked nose is a result of gravity pulling down and stretching the cartilage on the tip of the nose. The thin lips are caused by a loss of collagen and other plumping tissue in the lips. The pointed chin is caused by gravity and collagen loss.

110   112

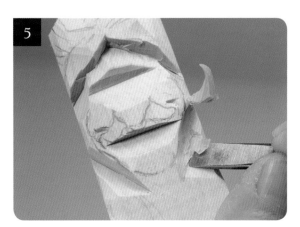

Separate the face from the background. Stop-cut along the face line with a carving knife. Carve up to the stop cut with a knife and a ⅜" #3 gouge to separate the face from the background.

Carve the eye sockets. Use a ¼" veiner to deepen the eye sockets. Then use the same tool to separate the eyebrows.

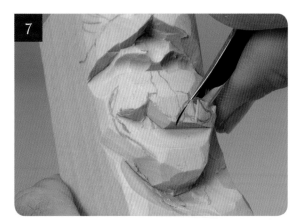

Rough in the nose. Stop-cut alongside the nose with a carving knife or a ⅜" #3 gouge. Cut up to the stop cut to separate the nose from the cheeks.

Rough in the sides of the face. Carve up alongside the face to the hair line with a ⅜" #3 gouge. Cut along the hair line to separate the hair from the sides of the face with the same tool.

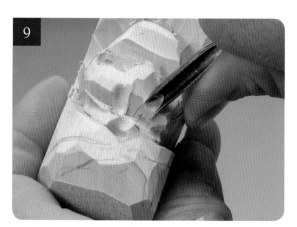

Separate the nose from the cheeks. Stop-cut alongside the nose and carve away the wood on the cheeks with a ⅜″ #3 gouge. Shape the sides of the nose with a ¼″ veiner.

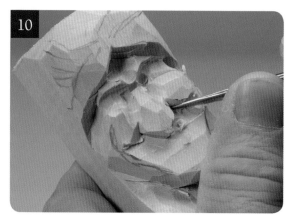

Shape the wings of the nose. Use a carving knife and a ⅜″ #3 gouge to shape the wings of the nose.

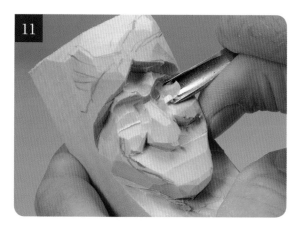

Deepen the eye sockets. Use a ⅜″ #9 gouge to deepen the eye sockets. Round the top of the cheeks down into the eye sockets using a ⅜″ #3 gouge upside down.

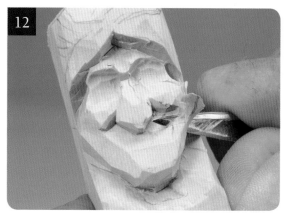

Thin the jowls. Carve along the sides of the face with a carving knife to create the thin pointed chin.

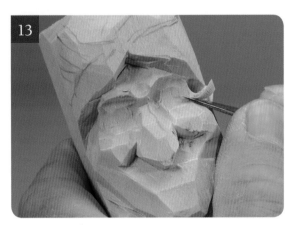

Finish roughing in the sides of the face. Carve the temple area and the end of the eye sockets using a carving knife.

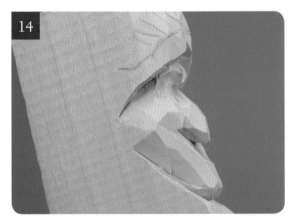

Add the hook to the tip of the nose. Use the carving knife to undercut the tip of the nose to create a hook shape.

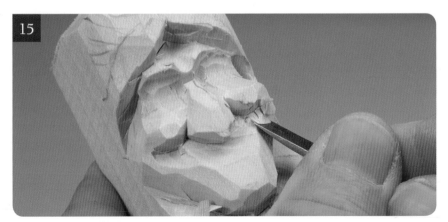

Accent the cheeks. Remove more wood from the area under the cheeks with a ⅜" #3 gouge to make the cheeks stick out more. The larger the cheeks, the more smiley the face looks.

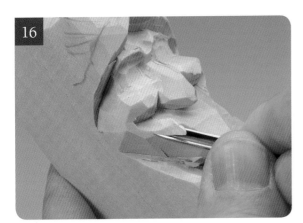

Thin the cheek and chin area. Use a ¼" veiner to carve grooves up alongside the face to the outside corners of the cheeks. This makes the face look like that of a thin old woman.

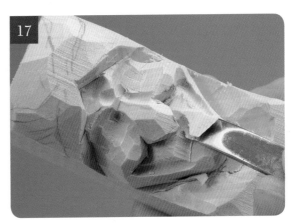

Deepen the area for the mouth. The pointed chin sticks out further than the mouth, so remove some wood in the mouth area with a ⅜" #3 gouge.

Rough in the mouth. Cut under the bottom lip with a small veiner to separate the bottom lip from the area under the lip. Stop-cut along the mouth lines with a carving knife.

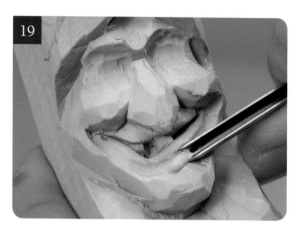

Finish shaping the mouth. Remove a bit of wood from inside the mouth to separate the mouth from the lips. Use a carving knife and a micro gouge to carve out the wood between the two teeth. Deepen the groove under the bottom lip, but make sure the bottom lip stays thin.

Shape the wings of the nose. Use a carving knife to remove a small wedge of wood from the sides of the nose to shape the wings of the nose. Carefully shape the bridge of the nose with a carving knife.

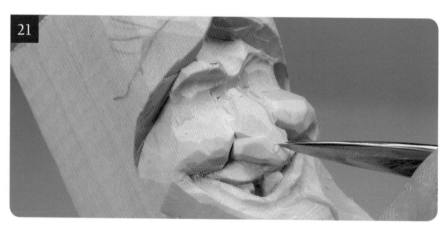

Add the wart to the nose. Stop-cut around the wart with a carving knife and relieve up to the stop cut carefully to separate the wart from the nose.

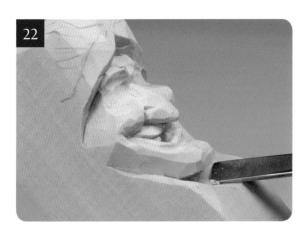

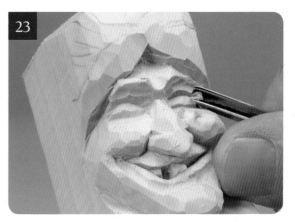

Undercut the pointed chin. Use a #3 gouge to carve under the chin so the chin sticks out from the rest of the block.

Separate the eyelids from the eye sockets. Carve along the outside edges of the eyelids with a ⅛" V-tool. This separates the eyelids from the eye sockets.

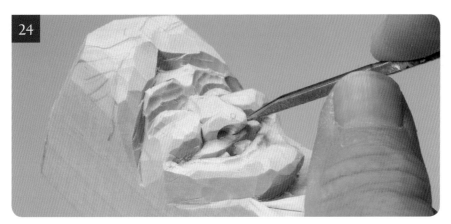

Carve the nostrils. Stab a small gouge into the nostril area. Then remove the chips with the same tool.

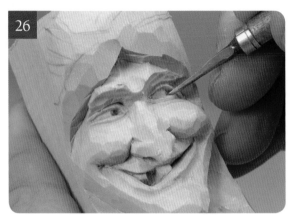

Carve the slitted eyes. Use a small V-tool to carefully carve along the edge of both eyelids. Carve carefully because you want only a thin slit. Use a carving knife to carefully cut up to the stop cuts and round the eyeball.

Carve the pupils. Use a micro gouge to carve a deep circle in the corners of the eyes to represent the pupils.

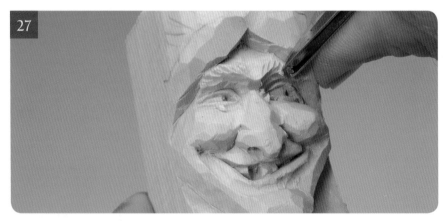

Carve the eyebrows. Use a ⅛" V-tool to carve a series of short grooves onto the brow line for the eyebrows.

Carve the crow's feet. Use a ⅛" V-tool to add a few wrinkles and crow's feet to the corners of the eyes.

Shape the hair. Use a V-tool to carve the long stringy hair. Carve out from or in to the part line to emphasize the separation of the hair at the part line.

Finish carving the hair. Carve some stringy hair coming down below the chin using a small V-tool. Clean out any fuzzies with a denture brush.

Ugly Face

A few specific features can turn an ordinary face into a face that speaks volumes in emotions and feelings. This angry face is a great example of how a few facial features, such as the squinty eyes and the frowning mouth, change the entire feel of the carving.

Like most carvings, the success of this depends on understanding how to carve the individual features. If you can't carve an eye, you can't change the eye from an ordinary eye to a squinting eye. Likewise, if you can't carve lips, you will struggle to carve a recognizable deep frown.

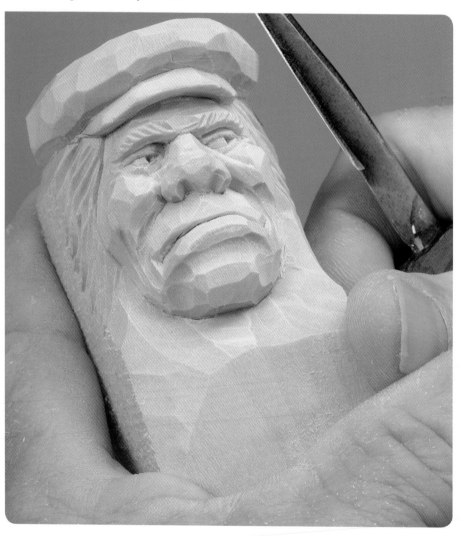

Sketch in the facial landmarks. Draw in the perimeter of the face and the cap. Draw in the eyebrows, eyes, nose, smile lines, and lips.

Rough in the cap. Round the top corners of the cap. Then carve a groove on either side to separate the top of the cap from the bill and face.

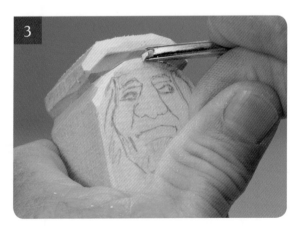

Separate the cap from the cap bill. Carve along the line separating the bill from the top of the cap with a ⅛" V-tool.

Shape the cap bill. Use a carving knife to shape the top of the cap bill.

Shape the temples. Carve up alongside the face with a ⅜" #3 gouge to shape the temples and separate the cap from the cap bill.

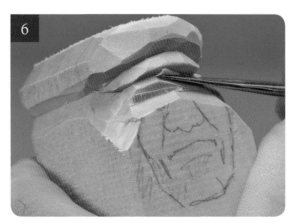

Separate the cap bill from the face. Stop-cut below the cap bill with a carving knife and taper the forehead up to the cap bill so the bill sticks out more than the face.

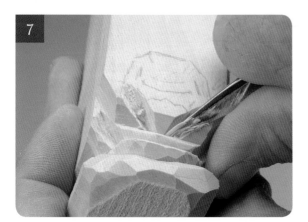

Rough out the sides of the nose. Stop-cut along the brow line with a carving knife and carve up to the stop cut as you carve along both sides of the nose to separate the nose from the rest of the face.

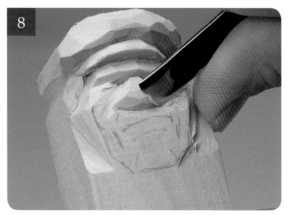

Rough out the rest of the nose. Make a stop cut under the nose with a ⅜" #3 gouge and cut up to the stop cut to outline the bottom of the nose. Use the same tool upside down to round the corners of the nose.

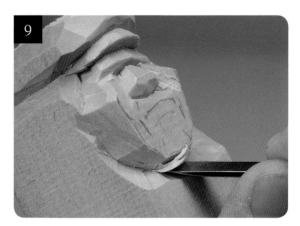

Rough out the sides of the face. Stop-cut along both sides of the face and carve up to the stop cuts to separate the face from the rest of the blank. Use a carving knife and a ⅜" #3 gouge. Round the face using the ⅜" #3 gouge upside down.

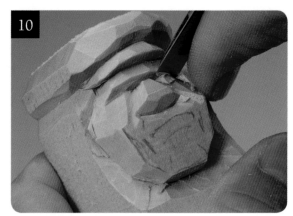

Deepen the eye sockets. Stab in along the brow line with a ⅜" #3 gouge and carve up to the stop cut.

Rough in the cheeks. Use a knife and a ⅜" #3 gouge to remove extra wood from the cheeks.

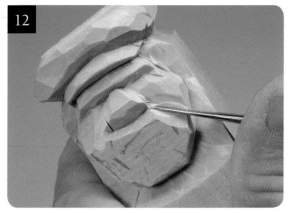

Add the smile lines. Use a carving knife to carve grooves from the nose downward to represent the smile lines.

Rough in the upper lip. Taper up from the top lip to the nose to shape the top of the upper lip. Use a carving knife.

Shape the edges of the face. Carve off the sides of the face using a carving knife. Smooth the sides of the cheeks and the chin area.

Carve under the lower lip. Use a ¼" veiner to carve a groove under the lower lip to separate the lower lip from the chin.

Deepen the smile lines. Use a 3mm veiner to deepen the smile lines and shape the edges of the top lip. Use a knife or skew chisel to rough in the wings of the nose.

Shape the outside edge of the face. Round and shape the outside edge of the face with a ⅜″ #3 gouge. Carve away the background wood so the face sticks up more.

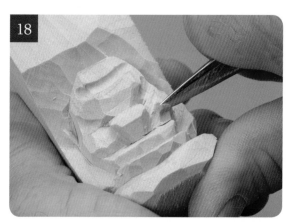

Deepen the inside corner of the eye sockets. Carve up from the cheeks into the eye sockets using a carving knife. This helps to separate the cheeks from the eye sockets.

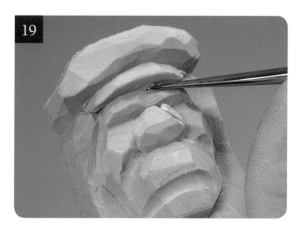

Carve the eyebrows. Use a ⅜″ #9 gouge to carve a small groove above the saddle of the nose between the eyebrows. Use a carving knife to remove a little wood above the eyebrows so the eyebrows stick out above the forehead.

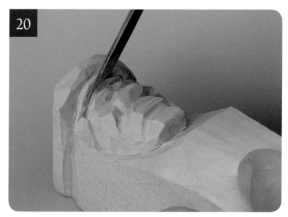

Undercut the cap bill. Use a ⅜″ #3 gouge to undercut the cap bill to separate the bill from the forehead. Round the top of the cap using a carving knife.

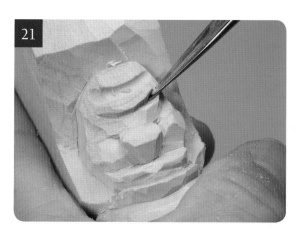

Shape the lips. Carve between the upper and lower lips using a carving knife.

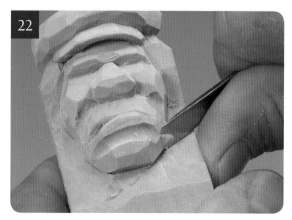

Shape the chin. Use a ⅜" #3 gouge upside down to round the bottom and sides of the chin.

Shape the corners of the mouth. Remove a small chip from the corner of the mouth to accent the frowning lips, using a carving knife.

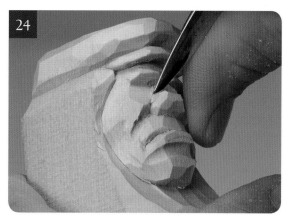

Refine the nose. Use a carving knife to shape the sides of the nose and the bridge of the nose.

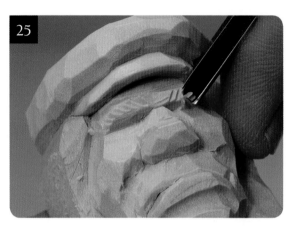

Carve the eyebrows. Carve a series of short grooves into the brow line with a ⅛" V-tool to represent eyebrows.

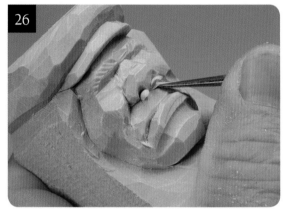

Carve the nostrils. Stab a small gouge into the bottom of the nose. Free the chips with a knife to shape the nostrils.

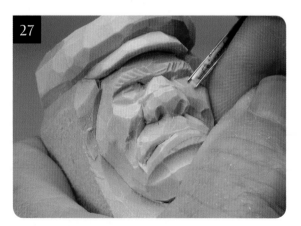

Carve the bags under the eyes. Use a micro gouge to carve a slight groove under the eye socket to represent the bags under the frowning eyes.

Carve the eyelids. Separate the eyelids from the eye socket by carving around the outer part of the eyelids with a ¹⁄₁₆" V-tool. Deepen the groove for the upper eyelid with a carving knife to create deep shadows. The deepest part of the eye is the corner closest to the nose. Round the eyelids with a carving knife.

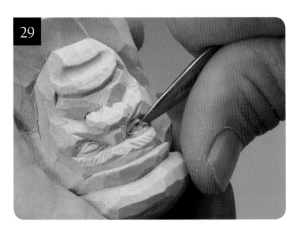

Separate the eyelids from the eyeballs. Sketch in the eyelids and stop-cut along the eyelids with a carving knife. Carve up to the stop cuts with a carving knife to round the eyeball under the eyelids.

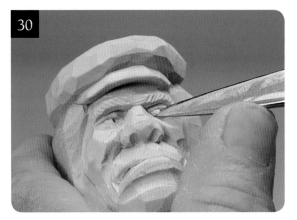

Carve the pupil. Remove a small chip from the corner of the eyeball with a carving knife to represent the pupil. This type of pupil and squinting eyes emphasize the frowning mean face.

Add the irises. Stab in with a micro gouge to create the outline of the iris.

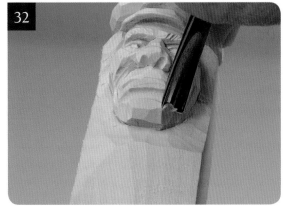

Shape the chin. Use a ⅜" #9 gouge to shape the chin and cheeks.

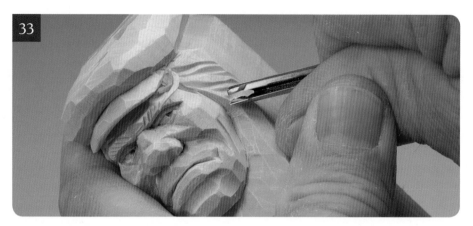

Carve the hair. Use a 1/8" V-tool to carve in the stringy hair. Make sure you carve random curved lines. Straight lines do not look realistic. Then add a few crow's feet alongside the eye sockets using the same tool.

Clean up any remaining rough areas. Use a denture brush to scrub out any fuzzies. Go over the carving with a sharp knife to clean up any rough cuts.

Wood Spirit

Wood spirits are popular carving subjects, and they are one of the easiest projects to carve. If you break it down to the elements, a wood spirit is really just an ugly old man carved with wild hair and a beard. I've found that the more ugly you make the face, the more people will like him.

In general, I prefer to carve wood spirits in found wood. The coarse nature of the found wood really emphasizes the feelings of the wood spirit. I consider carvings like this in ordinary wood wizards; a similar carving in found wood transforms into a wood spirit.

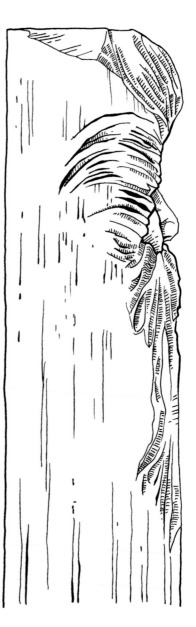

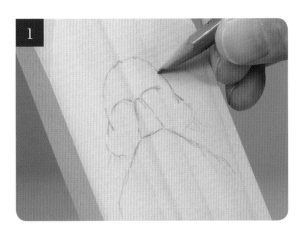

Rough out the blank. Round the top corners of the blank with a carving knife. Sketch in the major landmarks such as the forehead, eye sockets, nose, and mustache line.

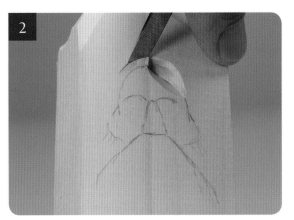

Separate the forehead from the hair. Stop-cut along the hairline and taper the forehead up to the stop cut. Use a ⅜" #3 gouge.

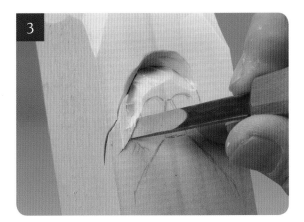

Separate the sides of the face from the blank. Stop-cut along the side of the face. Cut up to the stop cut to rough in the sides of the face and to separate the face from the blank. Use a carving knife and a ⅜" #3 gouge.

Separate the sides of the face from the blank. Stop-cut along the side of the face. Cut up to the stop cut to rough in the sides of the face and to separate the face from the blank. Use a carving knife and a ⅜" #3 gouge.

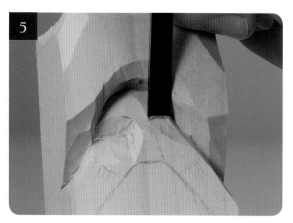

Separate the nose from the cheeks. Stop-cut alongside the nose and carve up to the brow line or down from the brow line, depending on the grain direction of the wood, with a ⅜" #3 gouge. This creates the deep craggy eye sockets and the tapered cheeks.

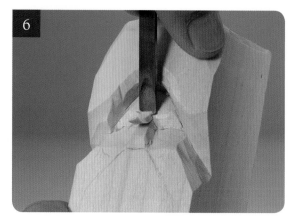

Carve the saddle of the nose. Cut up along the nose and down from the brow line with a ⅜" #3 gouge to shape the saddle of the nose.

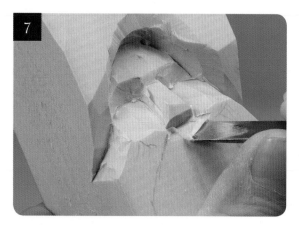

Rough out the bottom of the nose. Stop-cut along the bottom of the nose with a ⅜" #3 gouge and cut up to the stop cut to separate the nose from the mustache.

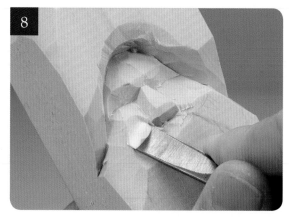

Separate the sides of the nose from the cheeks. Use a ⅜" #3 gouge and a skew chisel to relieve the wood from alongside the tip of the nose so the tip of the nose sticks out.

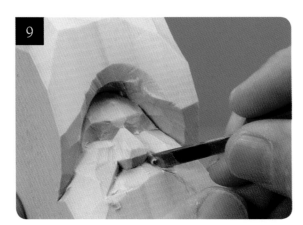

Carve the smile lines. Use a skew chisel and a carving knife to carve the grooves from the side of the nose down to the mustache. These grooves represent the smile lines.

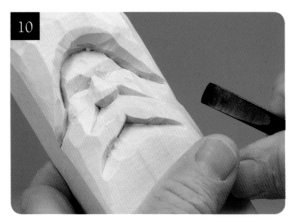

Separate the mustache from the beard. Stop-cut along the bottom of the mustache with a ⅜" #3 gouge. Carve up to the stop cut to separate the mustache from the beard.

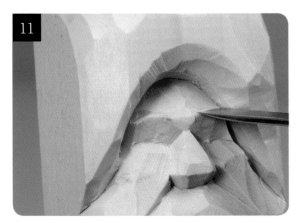

Separate the eyebrows from the forehead. Use a ⅜" #3 gouge to remove wood above the brow line so the brows stick out more.

Separate the eyebrows. Carve between the eyebrows with a ⅜" #9 gouge.

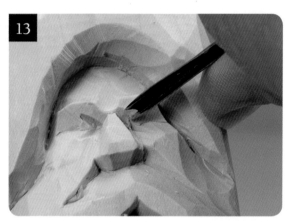

Deepen the inside corner of the eyes. Carve a sideways *V* in the corner of the eye closest to the nose using a ⅛" V-tool. This makes the inside corner the deepest part of the eye.

Carve the wings of the nose. Use a carving knife, a ⅜" #3 gouge, and a skew chisel to shape the wings of the nose. The wings of the nose start at the top of the smile lines.

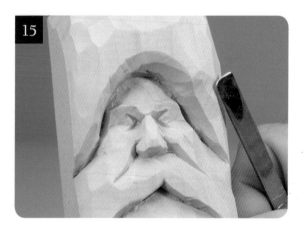

Refine the nose. Use a ⅜" #3 gouge upside down to refine the overall shape of the nose.

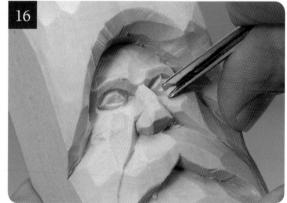

Separate the eyelids from the eye sockets. Carve along the outer part of the eyelids. Use a ⅛" V-tool. This separates the eyelids from the eye sockets. Draw in the top of the mustache.

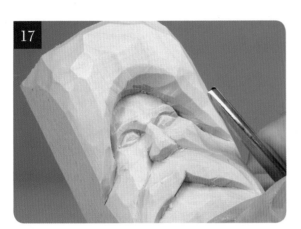

17

Carve the top of the mustache. Carve along the line with a ⅛" V-tool to separate the mustache from the cheeks. Sketch in the rough hair and mustache texture.

18

Carve the nostrils. Stab in with a micro gouge to shape the nostrils. Then cut the chip free with a carving knife.

19

Carve the eyebrows. Use a ⅛" V-tool to carve a series of short grooves on the brow line to represent eyebrows.

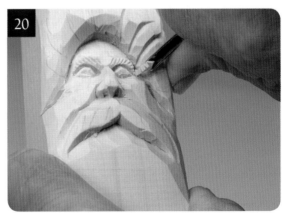

20

Carve the rough hair texture. Carve along the lines using a ⅛" V-tool. Make sure none of the lines are straight.

137

Carve the rough mustache texture. Carve short curved lines to start texturing the mustache with a ⅛" V-tool.

Continue separating the locks of hair. Use a carving knife and a ¼" #3 gouge upside down to break the hair up into large wild masses.

Shape the cheekbones. Use a carving knife and a ⅜" #3 gouge to carve away wood from under the cheekbones to make the cheekbones stick out.

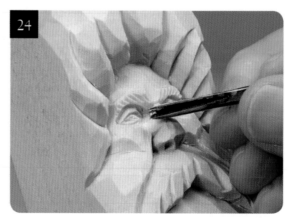

Separate the eyelids from the eyeball. Carve along the top and bottom eyelids with a ⅛" V-tool. This separates the eyelids from the eyeball.

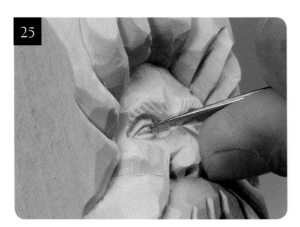

Deepen the stop cuts around the eyelids. Use a carving knife to deepen the stop cuts to make the lids look heavy.

Round the eyeball. Use a carving knife to cut up to the V-tool cuts. Round the eyeball between the eyelids.

Carve the pupils. Use a micro gouge to carve a pupil in the corner of the visible eyeball. You may need to use the tip of a carving knife to cut the chip free.

Break the locks of hair into smaller locks. Use a ¼"
veiner to break the large masses of hair into smaller locks.
Follow the established flow of the hair masses.

Rough texture the beard. Carve the beard into locks of
hair using a ¼" veiner. Do not carve any straight lines.

Carve the wild hair. Make a series of cuts with a ⅛" V-tool to represent the hair. Break all of the
hair masses into individual strands of hair. Do not carve straight lines. The curve of the individual
strands should match the curve of the lock.

More Great Carving Books from Fox Chapel Publishing

Lettering & Sign Carving Workbook
10 Skill-Building Projects for Carving and Painting Custom Signs
By Betty Padden

A contemporary look at a nostalgic craft with updated techniques and a fresh variety of styles for carving and painting signs for the home, summer cottage or basement bar.

ISBN: 978-1-56523-452-9
$19.95 • 160 Pages

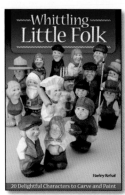

Whittling Little Folk
20 Delightful Characters to Carve and Paint
By Harley Refsal

A single carving knife and an afternoon is all that is needed to create one of the charming little characters in this book.

ISBN: 978-1-56523-518-2
$16.95 • 128 Pages

Making Wooden Fishing Lures
Carving and Painting Techniques that Really Catch Fish
By Rich Rousseau

Whether it is the thrill of catching a fish with a handmade lure or finding the perfect one to add to your collection, this book of 11 step-by-step projects with a collector's gallery will grab you hook, line and sinker.

ISBN: 978-1-56523-446-8
$19.95 • 176 Pages

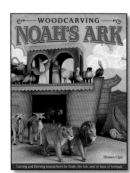

Woodcarving Noah's Ark
Carving and Painting Instructions for the Noah, the Ark, and 14 Pairs of Animals
By Shawn Cipa

Recreate the amazing adventure of Noah's Ark with a hand-carved wooden set that will be cherished for generations.

ISBN: 978-1-56523-477-2
$22.95 • 160 pages

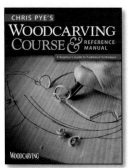

Chris Pye's Woodcarving Course & Reference Manual
A Beginner's Guide to Traditional Techniques
By Chris Pye

Ever dream of taking a one-on-one carving course with a master carver? This book is the next best thing. Chris Pye reveals the carving techniques he has honed over his many years as a woodcarver.

ISBN: 978-1-56523-456-7
$19.95 • 160 Pages

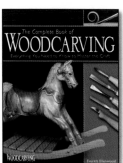

The Complete Book of Woodcarving
Everything You Need to Know to Master the Craft
By Everett Ellenwood

This comprehensive reference covers every classic style, along with power carving. Includes 9 projects and a helpful resource section.

ISBN: 978-1-56523-292-1
$27.95 • 288 pages

The Best of Woodcarving Illustrated

Expert tips, techniques, projects, and patterns from the pages of *Woodcarving Illustrated*.

Chip Carving
*Expert Techniques and
50 All-Time Favorite Projects*
By Editors of *Woodcarving Illustrated*
ISBN: 978-1-56523-449-9
$19.95 • 128 Pages

Relief Carving Projects & Techniques
Expert Techniques and 37 All-Time Favorite Projects & Patterns
By Editors of *Woodcarving Illustrated*
ISBN: 978-1-56523-558-8
$19.95 • 144 Pages

Power Carving Manual
Tools, Techniques, and 16 All-Time Favorite Projects
By Editors of *Woodcarving Illustrated*
ISBN: 978-1-56523-450-5
$19.95 • 152 Pages

Caricature Carving
Expert Techniques and 30 All-Time Favorite Projects
By Editors of *Woodcarving Illustrated*

ISBN: 978-1-56523-474-1
$19.95 • 144 Pages

Woodcarver's Guide to Sharpening, Tools and Setting Up Shop
Expert Tips and Techniques
By Editors of *Woodcarving Illustrated*
ISBN: 978-1-56523-475-8
$19.95 • 144 Pages

WOODCARVING
ILLUSTRATED BOOKS

In addition to being a leading source of woodworking books and DVDs, Fox Chapel also publishes *Woodcarving Illustrated*. Released quarterly, it delivers premium projects, expert tips and techniques from today's finest carvers, and in-depth information about the latest tools, equipment, and materials.

Subscribe Today!
Woodcarving Illustrated: **888-506-6630**
www.FoxChapelPublishing.com

Harold Enlow Study Stick Kits

In addition to the in-depth instructions, quality photos, and crisp patterns inside the
Carving Faces Workbook, Harold created companion study sticks for each project.
Each kit includes a study stick and booklet version of the instructions in this book.

**Wood Spirit
Study Stick Kit**

ISBN: 978-1-56523-584-7
$19.95

**Eyes and Lips
Study Stick Kit**

ISBN: 978-1-56523-579-3
$19.95

**Female Face
Study Stick Kit**

ISBN: 978-1-56523-575-5
$19.95

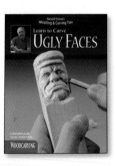

**Noses and Hair
Study Stick Kit**

ISBN: 978-1-56523-580-9
$19.95

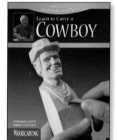

Cowboy Study Stick Kit

ISBN: 978-1-56523-576-2
$19.95

Ear Study Stick Kit

ISBN: 978-1-56523-581-6
$19.95

**Native American Chief
Study Stick Kit**

ISBN: 978-1-56523-577-9
$19.95

**Ugly Faces
Study Stick Kit**

ISBN: 978-1-56523-583-0
$19.95

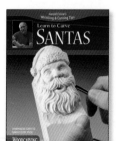

**Santas Study
Stick Kit**

ISBN: 978-1-56523-578-6
$19.95

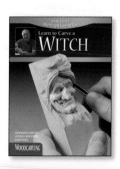

**Holiday Caricatures
Study Stick Kit**

(stick features witch +5 other faces)

ISBN: 978-1-56523-582-3
$19.95

Look for These Kits at Your Local Specialty Retailer
To order direct, call **800-457-9112** or visit *www.FoxChapelPublishing.com*

By mail, please send check or money order + .99 per book and $3.00 for S&H to: Fox Chapel Publishing, 1970 Broad Street, East Petersburg, PA 17520